Additional Praise for *Never Dull*

"As the newspaper business slowly sinks into the digital sea, Larry Ames delivers a terrific salute to how life was when sportswriters prowled the earth and projectiles flew through the air toward end zones and home plates and fingers moved across typewriters and deadlines loomed in the distance. Great stuff from a guy who saw it all. Makes you wish it would stay the same forever."

—Leigh Montville, N.Y. Times best-selling author of nine books on sports personalities, former Boston Globe columnist

"Larry Ames was the first boss I had in journalism, and the one I learned the most from about work ethic and how to get to the bottom of a story, no matter what the obstacles. In his descriptive memoir, readers will learn as much as I did and more about one of the most determined people in the history of sports journalism. His memoir is full of behind-the-scenes anecdotes regarding the pursuit of stories on legends like Sparky Anderson, Larry Bird, Will McDonough, and Doug Flutie – just to name a few."

—Ian Browne, Boston Red Sox beat reporter, MLB.com, author of "Idiots Revisited"

NEVER DULL

NEVER DULL

A SPORTS JOURNALIST'S
41-YEAR ADVENTURE

LARRY AMES

Redwood Publishing, LLC

Published by Redwood Publishing, LLC

To book Larry to speak at an event, or to reach out to him directly, please contact: authorlames@gmail.com. To reach out to the publisher, please contact: info@redwooddigitalpublishing.com

Proudly printed in the United States of America

ISBN Paperback: 978-0-9981760-3-1
ISBN eBook: 978-0-9981760-5-5

Library of Congress Control Number: 2017945562

Designed by Redwood Publishing, LLC
Cover Design: Michelle Manley

*To my patient wife, Bunny, and my son, David,
who often took a back seat to a husband and father
who spent much time away from family to pursue a
four-decade career in sports journalism.*

CONTENTS

SECTION TWO—THE EXPERIENCES

ACKNOWLEDGMENTS

Without the encouragement and support of my great friend, Ritch Eich, and my wife, Bunny, this memoir would never have been possible.

The path to publishing a book is daunting for a first-time author, but my task was made incredibly easier because of the talent and patience of Redwood Publishing's Sara Stratton.

FOREWORD

WHEN YOU'RE YOUNG, AMBITIOUS, AND BOLD AND HAVE already had a modicum of success at nineteen years old, you think you can do anything. You approach everything without fear—and sometimes without a—gasp—filter. As I look back on those years, I smile at the carefree attitude and the confidence that nothing would ever stand in the way.

One afternoon in the spring of 1992, I placed a call to *The Boston Globe*. I was in the middle of my freshman year at Northeastern University, and I had applied for one of the coveted co-op positions in The Globe sports department. My interview had been scheduled, but I decided to reach out to the high school sports editor, Larry Ames, to make an impression before I came in.

We have varying accounts of the conversation, but, according to Larry, I predicted that he was going to hire me and I told him why. I don't know if I ever made such a brash prediction, but I guess I made an impression.

When you're nineteen, you don't really think about mentors. I approached everything with hard work and determination and believed in my heart of hearts that I could outwork and outwill anyone. If I did that nothing could stop me from being successful. Along the way, I quickly discovered—though I didn't realize it at the time—that you needed much more than that. You needed someone to take you under his or her wing, cheer your successes, and help you learn from your mistakes. You needed someone to guide you along.

Larry Ames was a tough man with a unique set of rules. "Amesisums" we called them. Follow the rules and work hard and you'd be on his good side. Don't, and you'd incur his wrath. He hated those who were lazy (and carpetbaggers, but that's another story). Larry must have seen something in me from the start. I worked hard and didn't complain about his rules, although I did find some of them a bit ridiculous. He also had a laundry list of sayings, many which still ring in my head all the time.

You don't assume, you know!

We're not clock watchers. You leave when you're done!

If you don't know assssskkkkkkkk!

Never wear a hat inside.

No excuses! Get the job done!

I spent three-plus years working under Larry at The Globe. I never worked harder or learned more than I did during that time. Larry taught me how to work, how to figure things out on my own, and he pushed me harder than I've ever been pushed. I needed it and wouldn't be the successful journalist (and person) I am today without him.

Because of Larry, I never forgot where I came from. He loved high school sports and so do I. Covering schools helped me form a foundation that has carried me to the top of my profession. Figure out how to chase down the losing coach running for a bus or file in 15 minutes amidst a group of screaming teenagers and no task seems insurmountable.

I've been to eighteen Final Fours, but nothing will ever top the two-day WPI marathon, during which I covered eight state championship games in two days at Worcester Polytechnic Institute. There were two field hockey finals on Friday night and six state championship soccer games the following day. If you could do that and manage to leave still standing, you can do anything. It was a badge of honor I still hold proudly.

It wasn't until I earned my dream job at *Sports Illustrated* a few years later that I realized what I had in a mentor. I had made it to the big leagues, the pinnacle of my profession, and I was better trained and better prepared than any of my contemporaries. Larry Ames prepared me better than any classroom, any textbook, writer, or editor could have prepared anyone. I took everything he said to heart and absorbed it. Unconsciously I knew he saw something special in me and I was determined to live up to and exceed my potential.

In fact, I had taken on so much of Larry that The Globe sports copy desk started nicknaming me Larry's biological son. It wasn't that I was brown nosing. I was so driven, and I recognized that Larry could help me get where I wanted to go. The fact that he believed in me was the first step, and then he never let up in pushing me. Never let me slide. I didn't appreciate that at the time, but I do now.

Not only did Larry help me reach my goals and dreams, he also inspired me to become a mentor myself. Over the years I hired and mentored scores of interns and young employees. I helped them develop, giving them the knowledge, advice, and the push they needed to reach their potential. For eight years, I taught undergraduate, graduate, and law students. Nothing gives me more pleasure than teaching and inspiring.

I've often wondered and asked myself, "What do you do when you get your dream job at twenty-three?" The answer is you keep pushing yourself to move forward, to become a better version of yourself, to do what you never thought was possible. Last year, I decided to leave Sports Illustrated, where I rose to executive editor, after twenty years. My next step is going to involve teaching, mentoring, and innovation. It is my true calling.

I never would have realized this if it hadn't been for Larry. Over the years, our relationship has taken a different direction. Instead of pushing me, he took on the role of a proud father, praising me for my accomplishments, expressing pride in the person I have become, and cautioning me to prioritize and enjoy life. Like everything he's ever said to me, I've taken his advice to heart and it's made me a better person.

What's a mentor? Someone who sees something in you and brings out the best. Someone who supports you through good times and bad and helps you become a better version of yourself. For all those reasons and more, Larry Ames is the best mentor I could have ever asked for. He will forever be *my* mentor.

—B.J. Schecter

Preface

An Unlikely Prospect
To Be A Sports Journalist

TODAY, WE LIVE IN A WORLD WHERE YOUNGSTERS ARE ferried all over the landscape for soccer, baseball, basketball, hockey, football, tennis, golf, or lacrosse practice. Others spend countless hours studying a musical instrument, learning to become an actor or dancer, or becoming a games wizard on countless computer games. Geniuses pursue academic knowledge.

These activities help nurture young people to develop skills that steer them in a direction to become savvy, contributing members of society.

In September 1944, when I was born at Massachusetts Memorial Hospital in Boston, there was little opportunity for a youngster.

The Great Depression was followed by World War II. In America, money was poured into the war effort, and there wasn't any money for much of anything else.

I didn't see my father, Ernest J. (Jack) Ames, until he returned from the front lines of Germany in 1945.

I grew up in Boston (in the Blue Hill Avenue section of Dorchester, a largely Jewish ghetto populated mostly by immigrant families who arrived in the United States from Eastern Europe).

Franklin Field in Dorchester was one of the largest open spaces in America. It had a gravel track and several baseball diamonds, but Little League didn't arrive until 1956, when I was eleven and, never having played the sport, I was assigned to the minor leagues.

The basketball court had no nets and broken backboards, and the eight tennis courts had no nets and were full of cracks with weeds growing. There was no swimming pool, only ground sprinklers which were shut down in the early 1950s because of the polio epidemic.

The only pristine section of the field was the bocce court, and most of the players were elderly Italian immigrants.

The major activity in the field was cricket, which I often watched for hours, although I did not know the rules of the sport.

The area did have the Franklin Park golf course, but the course was never in good shape. Even though the public course was inexpensive, it was still too much for the average Bostonian.

So how did I ever develop an interest in sports and sports journalism?

My Independence Day came on July 1, 1952, when my mother, Yetta, informed my sister and me that she had divorced our father.

I started going to Red Sox games at Fenway Park and watched the Bruins and Celtics at Boston Garden. When I wasn't at the games, I listened to nationally known broadcasters Johnny Most (Celtics), Curt Gowdy (Red Sox), and Fred Cusick (Bruins). I often fell asleep listening to games on my transistor radio.

At the same time, I started reading the Boston newspapers. There were six Boston daily papers in 1952, and there were days when I read four or five of them. The papers each cost a nickel, the same price as a cup of coffee.

I admired many of the writers, some of whom I would eventually work with, and others whom I met covering assignments.

During high school, I worked as a stock boy at Kenley's women's clothing store in the Fields Corner section of Dorchester, and I started saving for college with my 75 cents an hour wage.

However, in March 1961, I developed a virus of unknown origin. I was admitted to Beth Israel Hospital in Boston with a temperature of 107.4 degrees. I was semi-conscious for eleven days, and I had around-the-clock nurses.

On the day I was released from the hospital, I was wheeled into an auditorium full of doctors who were briefed on my illness. I had no right to be alive, but somehow I survived.

What didn't survive was my college fund, which was wiped out by my illness.

When I graduated from Dorchester High, I enrolled at Newton Junior College, where I became the manager of the basketball and baseball teams.

Part of my duties was calling *The News-Tribune*, the newspaper covering Newton and Waltham, with the team results.

In January 1965, I received a call from John Vellante of *The News-Tribune*.

"You do a great job calling in scores. Would you be interested in taking scores here in the office?" Vellante asked.

Thus began my journalistic career. I was hired full time in December 1966.

I was fortunate to work at *The News-Tribune*, considered one of the top training papers in the area. I had several excellent mentors at The Tribune and at *The Boston Herald*, where I worked part-time from 1967 to 1972. I had overcome many obstacles en route to my successful career.

And although the road was rocky and uncertain, I appreciated the hurdles, because it made me appreciate my opportunities all the more.

INTRODUCTION

MOST SPORTS BOOKS FEATURE ATHLETES, THEIR STATISTICS, championships, titles, etc.

I spent four decades as a sports journalist. For half of my career I was a writer and copy editor. The second half of my career I was an assistant sports editor or sports editor who also wrote commentary.

Sports writing has changed considerably in the last century. Sports sections often focused on results and statistics. Features were secondary because, other than newspapers, there were few options to provide scores, standings, and summaries.

Even before the Internet, when more games were televised and cable expanded, there was a newspaper movement to write game stories that told more than the results. Readers already knew the score, so the focus of game stories shifted to analysis and how the game affected today and what it meant for tomorrow, next week, or next month.

The Internet changed that focus even more. People wanted to know "the story behind the story."

More columns and commentary appeared, and there were more human interest features.

As a writer and editor, I've always believed that the journey was far more interesting than a score or statistic.

I arrived at *The Boston Globe* in June 1978, and the following January I was named the newspaper's school sports editor. All previous school sports editors were writers who supervised the paper's college interns who wrote for the school sports pages.

My task was to hire, train, and supervise young writers and have them produce metropolitan newspaper level copy. The Globe's School Sports pages provided an opportunity to go beyond the norm. Instead of writing a feature on a stud football player or a basketball superstar, we were more interested in athletes who exhibited talents off the field as well. That focus led us to create a Scholar-Athlete program in 1986.

Features on coaches didn't always focus on X's and O's. We did a feature on Swampscott football coaching legend Stan Bondelevitch, who, we learned, was an accomplished chef and prepared his Thanksgiving turkey two days before the traditional holiday game with Marblehead. We also printed coach Bondelevitch's Polish kielbasa stuffing recipe.

The Globe's sports copy desk was critical of the story, but I knew it was well received when a reader called and asked if Italian sausage could be substituted for the kielbasa.

Our coverage produced suggestions from readers who recognized that our pages were open to interesting newspaper copy.

I covered the Massachusetts Interscholastic Athletic Association, the state's governing body for high school sports, because we wanted to inform our readers what was going on with the legislative body that affected everything to do with athletes, programs, and policies.

Our coverage was often critical. I took the MIAA to the state attorney general when I believed it violated the state open meeting law. I challenged the MIAA's assertion that its records were not public. I won rulings in both cases.

Because politics is unavoidable in high school sports, I tackled a lot of issues, including budget and program cuts to high school athletics, particularly in the city of Boston.

The building where track athletes practiced and competed was demolished in 1958. I championed the building of a state track facility to replace it.

Despite a myriad of ups and downs over eleven years and more than 100 stories and critical columns, the Reggie Lewis Track and Athletic Center opened in 1995, more than 38 years after a replacement building was first proposed. The path to success is a story unto itself.

At The Globe, I was a very small fish in a very big pond. The paper's sports section was considered among the best, if not the best, in the entire country. Its writers were superstars known nationally and internationally.

In my career, I had the opportunity to dabble occasionally on the professional and college scenes. Some of the stories in this book describe in detail the people and the adventures.

There is much more to putting out a daily newspaper than writing and editing stories. There is the human side of sports, and this book chronicles the many decisions and many paths that were followed before a story appeared in the newspaper.

The stories of my experiences in making the decisions to do the stories, the twists and turns of setting up and conducting interviews, and the many surprises along the way are what make this book different.

In the chapter on Sparky Anderson, my interactions with him occurred in 1975, 2000, 2006, and 2007. In my first experience, I was a writer covering the World Series in Boston. Subsequently, I covered his induction into the Baseball Hall of Fame as an assistant sports editor in California. In my final experience with Anderson, as a retiree, I successfully nominated his induction into the South Dakota Hall of Fame.

Being an editor as well as a writer gave me a greater understanding of a great story. In many respects, how the stories landed in the paper were far more interesting than the stories themselves.

I was fortunate to have been trained by incredible mentors, and I became a mentor to the college interns who worked in The Globe sports department and wrote for the School Sports pages. A chapter deals with the the successes of many "Ames graduates."

One section of the book deals with some of the personalities I've encountered. Some of the people mentioned in this book are well known; many others may not be known universally, but all of their stories are incredible.

Another section describes my relationships and experiences with people ranging from governors and mayors to boxing promoters and major league managers and coaches.

The third section offers commentary and includes a commencement address I made and a column on my last day of work.

The fourth section, This and That, is a long list of short, but interesting, experiences and comments.

SECTION ONE
THE PEOPLE

George 'Sparky' Anderson

The first time I met Sparky Anderson was on October 21, 1975. That night I didn't really meet him, but I was among dozens of media crowded into the Cincinnati Reds locker room at Fenway Park. But I did get to know him significantly better in 2000, 2006, and 2007.

I was at Fenway to cover Game 6 of the 1975 World Series, considered by many to be the best game ever played in baseball's postseason classic.

Carlton Fisk's 12th-inning home run at 12:34 a.m. had given the Boston Red Sox a 7-6 victory in a thriller that lasted four hours and a minute.

My assignment that night for *The Salem News* was to write two stories from a Cincinnati viewpoint for the next afternoon's paper.

World Series Game 6 was my second marathon that day.

The first part of my marathon that day began with my work day at the News which started at 5:45 a.m. I always awakened at 5 a.m. and drove from my West Peabody home to the newspaper's office in Salem.

I was a sports reporter/editor at the paper, covering games, writing features, and editing and laying out the sports section.

On days when I worked a split shift, I often came home around 11 a.m. and took a short nap. I didn't take a nap that day because I had to pick up sports editor Bill Kipouras at 4 p.m. and head into Boston to cover the game, the second part of my marathon.

By the time I had interviewed Anderson and many of the Reds, it was past 3 a.m., and it was time to head home. Kipouras asked me if I would mind driving *Boston Record-American* columnist Larry Claflin to his home in Marblehead. After I dropped Claflin off, I took Kipouras to his downtown Peabody home. He wanted to sleep for a couple of hours before coming into the office to write his column and a sidebar from the Red Sox perspective.

I looked at my watch, and it was 5 a.m., time to get up, but I was already up and it was time to go to the office.

I wrote my two Reds stories, edited all the sports copy, and laid out and made up the sports section in the composing room.

I arrived home at noon, completing a thirty-one-hour day.

My wife, Bunny, told me she had experienced a difficult night of her own. While I was at Fenway, our infant son, David, was ill and had spent a good part of the night at the doctor's office.

Ironically, David's illness was not the only medical experience in the Ames family when I was covering Sparky Anderson.

After covering World Series Game 7, won by Cincinnati 4-3, I didn't see Sparky Anderson for twenty-five years.

I joined *The Boston Globe* as a sports copy editor in 1978 and became the school sports editor in 1979. I was promoted to assistant sports editor/schools in 1983, and I took a buyout from The Globe in 1994. In April 1996, I became assistant sports editor at The Ventura County Star in California.

Ventura County is a hotbed of sports. In the two Summer Olympics during my ten years at The Star, the county had ten

U.S. Olympians at the Sydney and Athens Olympics. States like North and South Dakota each had two Olympians.

In 2000, Marion Jones was the most famous female track athlete in the world. She had run track at Thousand Oaks High and was the Gatorade National Runner of the Year twice.

David Lassen, The Star's columnist, had covered Jones in high school and was scheduled to cover her again in Sydney for The Star and for all the Scripps Howard newspapers across the United States.

Lassen had worked for the *Thousand Oaks News Chronicle* before it merged with The Star. During Lassen's time with the paper he had almost exclusively covered Sparky Anderson, who lived in Thousand Oaks. However, it was decided that Lassen was going to cover Jones in U.S. Olympic Track Trials in Sacramento.

There was one other major local sports story that week, and I agreed to cover that big story—Sparky Anderson's induction into baseball's Hall of Fame.

Two weeks before his July induction, I arrived at Sparky's house for a two-hour interview. My story would appear in the paper the Sunday before the induction.

Anderson compiled a 2,194-1,834 record as a major league manager, winning two World Series for Cincinnati (1975, 1976) and one with the Detroit Tigers (1984). He was the first manager to win Series titles in each league, and since then only one other manager, Tony LaRussa, has equaled that feat.

Anderson's Major League career was very short. His only full season in the Majors was 1951 when he was the starting second baseman for the Philadelphia Phillies.

So when Reds General Manager Bob Howsam selected him to manage the Reds in 1969, Anderson was shocked.

"I would not have hired me as manager," Sparky said. It was a typical comment from a man who was always humble.

In the two-hour interview I learned a lot about the man.

My first question was, "Sparky, you've won World Series titles and numerous other major awards. What makes it so special that you're about to enter the Baseball Hall of Fame?"

"It's because I will be the first South Dakotan in the Hall of Fame," he said.

Anderson was born in Bridgewater, South Dakota, but his father couldn't find work and moved the family to Southern California. However, Anderson always felt he was a South Dakotan and maintained close ties to his native state.

In 2007, I would accompany Anderson back to his home state as an inductee of the South Dakota Hall of Fame.

In contrast to the millions of dollars in salaries paid to players and managers now, Anderson did not make a fortune from baseball.

"Without my father-in-law's donation of $8,000, my wife and I would not have been able to afford our house," he said.

I had planned to take my wife, Bunny, to the Baseball Hall of Fame induction weekend. Because my job as a sports journalist involved many long hours and days, I always tried to involve my wife in some of my coverage.

We planned to fly to Hartford, to spend a night with my

wife's brother, Stan Zwirn, and his wife, Gloria. Two days before the flight to Hartford, my wife complained of stomach pains. She saw the doctor the next day, and at 3 a.m. the day of the flight, my wife said she did not feel well and couldn't go. I said I would cancel my trip, but she urged me to go without her. "You need to be there. This is too big a story for you not to be there."

I flew to Connecticut, and upon arriving in Hartford, I learned Bunny was scheduled to have her appendix out. At dinner, I called the hospital and found out that the surgery was a success. That would not be the only hospital visit that weekend for a member of the Ames family.

I was unable to get hotel accommodations near the Hall of Fame in Cooperstown, so I made reservations at a Marriott in Albany. I drove to Cooperstown Saturday morning to pick up my credentials and to cover the Hall of Fame Saturday news conference.

I found a parking space a few blocks from the Hall of Fame, locked the car and started walking. A few steps later, I tripped on a raised sidewalk and fell, hurting my right wrist and tearing my pants. Since my car was close by, I changed pants and then headed to the Hall.

Once I secured my credentials, I found a trainer, who cleaned my wrist and wrapped an ace bandage on my wrist.

When the news conference ended, I drove to Albany and wrote two stories in my hotel room. I filed the first story, but while sending my notebook, my laptop died.

I resurrected my notes, called The Star and dictated my story over the phone. I also arranged for a reporter to take dictation on Sunday after the Hall of Fame ceremonies.

It was nine at night and I hadn't eaten since breakfast in Connecticut, so I went to the hotel restaurant and had a steak.

I chose to go to bed rather than head to the hospital emergency room, figuring that on a Saturday night there might be a long wait.

I awakened at 6 a.m. and headed to the hospital, where x-rays proved negative for a break, but I did have a severe sprain.

After breakfast, I drove to Cooperstown to find a parking space. I pulled into a church parking lot, paid my fee, and parked the car. When I left the lot, I asked to speak to the church pastor. I told him I needed to use his phone to dictate three stories once the ceremonies were over. I promised to make the calls collect, and I told him I would send the church a check to express my thanks for helping me.

The Hall of Fame ceremonies had a definite Cincinnati flavor and, for me, very reminiscent of my World Series experience in 1975. Fisk was an inductee, as was the Reds' Tony Perez. Anderson was selected by the Veterans Committee (now called the Eras Committee), as was Bid McPhee, another Cincinnati player who was also chosen by the Veterans Committee. The broadcasting inductee made it a near clean sweep for Cincinnati—Reds announcer Marty Brenneman.

Even one of the vendors on Main St. provided Cincinnati fans with more excitement. The disgraced Pete Rose, banned from all baseball activities, had a booth signing autographs, and the sport's all-time hits leader did a brisk business selling his autograph.

Anderson was the first inductee to speak, and Sparky admonished the pro-Cincinnati crowd that had booed Commissioner Bud Selig when he made introductory remarks.

"Bud Selig is one of the finest people I've met in all of baseball," said Anderson. His comments were typical of Anderson, who always spoke his mind.

One revelation during the ceremony was a charity that Anderson had created. While managing in Detroit, Anderson founded a charitable organization, Catch (Caring Athletes Teamed for Children's and Henry Ford Hospitals) in 1987. The charity helps provide care for ill children whose parents couldn't pay for health care.

I didn't see Sparky for another six years, but I attended a weekend celebration of the naming of Cal Lutheran University's baseball field in Sparky's honor in January 2006. Sparky lived barely a half-mile from the college and was a big supporter of the university's baseball team.

I retired as sports editor of The Star in May 2006, finishing a forty-one-year career in sports journalism, but later that year Sparky Anderson returned to my life. Actually, it was I who returned to Sparky's life.

My wife and I were barely a week into our eleven-week, thirty-six-state cross-country trip when we passed a sign in Chamberlain, South Dakota, that read: South Dakota Hall of Fame this exit. We were ahead of schedule for the day, so we stopped and toured the Hall for a solid hour and a half. We noticed that War hero and first AFL Commissioner Joe

Foss was an inductee, as were Mary Hart and Tom Brokaw.

Even Carroll Hardy, a backup outfielder for my hometown Boston Red Sox, was in the Hall. Hardy's only claim to fame was he was the only player to ever pinch-hit for the great Ted Williams.

I didn't see Sparky's name among the inductees, so I inquired at the front desk if I had somehow missed his plaque. I was informed by executive director Todd Lindquist that Sparky had been nominated twice, but hadn't been selected.

I couldn't imagine Carroll Hardy in a Hall of Fame and Sparky Anderson among the missing.

Lindquist told me that retired Sioux Falls sportswriter John Egan had been the person behind Anderson's nomination push. I told Lindquist I was just beginning a long trip, but asked if he would have Egan contact me.

Almost two months later, as my wife and I were about to start a wine tasting in Branson, Missouri, my cell phone rang. It was Egan, who told me of his unsuccessful efforts to get Sparky into the South Dakota Hall of Fame. "Sparky's in the South Dakota Sports Hall of Fame, but not in the main Hall of Fame."

I told Egan I would send a note to the nominating committee when I returned to California. "Perhaps," I said, "an outsider's nomination might help Sparky."

We returned from our cross-country trip the Monday of Thanksgiving. I spent two days putting together a letter of nomination on behalf of Sparky to the South Dakota Hall of Fame.

I started my letter by relating my interview with Sparky before he entered the Baseball Hall of Fame, noting his pride at being the first South Dakotan to be so honored.

It's hard to say if that approach or my outsider's view of one of baseball's icons made a difference, but in April 2007, I received word that Sparky had been selected for induction.

In June, I received an invitation to the Hall of Fame's induction weekend in September.

Upon arrival in Chamberlain to start the induction weekend, I was informed as Sparky's nominator I would explain to the gathering how I came to nominate Sparky. I was one of fifteen speakers to introduce inductees in categories such as business, government, entertainment, etc.

The highlight for me that evening was sharing the honor with Sparky by unfurling his Hall of Fame plaque.

The next day included a luncheon awards ceremony and a festive evening dinner.

I particularly enjoyed many private moments with Sparky that weekend, quite a contrast to our first "meeting" at the World Series in 1975.

Sparky Anderson died on November 4, 2010 at age seventy-six.

The Incomparable Will McDonough

As a sports journalist for more than four decades, I met hundreds of thousands of people. No one compares in magnitude to Will McDonough, my former Boston Globe colleague.

McDonough was a sports reporter and columnist for The Globe, but he was a giant in every way and much more than just a writer. He championed and created charities and was always willing to lend a hand to anyone who needed it.

He was a son of Southie, growing up in the Old Colony project of South Boston and remaining fearlessly loyal to anyone from the neighborhood.

McDonough was the campaign manager for Billy Bulger, running Bulger's first campaign for public office, a successful run for state representative in 1960. Bulger went on to become the powerful president of the Massachusetts state senate and later was president of the University of Massachusetts.

And, yes, Will was a friend of Billy's brother, notorious gangster James "Whitey" Bulger.

McDonough's main beat was pro football, and no one in the country had more exclusives than McDonough.

In 1983, McDonough wrote that Herschel Walker, the great Georgia running back, was going to snub the NFL and sign a contract to play for the New Jersey Generals of the USFL.

The morning the story broke, there were denials all over the country, which brought Globe editor Matt Storin racing down to the sports department to confront McDonough, whose desk in the sports department was right in front of mine.

"I want a retraction," Storin barked at McDonough. "Not one other person in the country is writing this."

Willie's first reaction had to be: "They're all wrong."

For minutes, McDonough and Storin exchanged harsh words, and I sat there wondering what I would do in the event a fight broke out. Fortunately, the verbal battle ended, and McDonough had the last word when his exclusive turned out to be right. A pro football writer once told me a story about an NFL meeting in Phoenix.

"We were all waiting for NFL commissioner Paul Tagliabue to finish his round of golf so we could ask him some questions. When Tagliabue walked up to the 18th green, who was playing in his foursome? McDonough, of course. No one had more contacts in sports than Willie," the writer bemoaned to me.

It went deeper than that. When Pete Rozelle either summoned other writers to his suite (only a few covered the NFL in those days) or walked down to meet them, who was already with him? McDonough.

Writers are rarely friends with sports team owners, but Willie had two close friends in Oakland Raiders owner Al Davis and Cleveland Browns owner Art Modell, so it was not hard to figure out how McDonough always trumped his colleagues when it came to NFL news.

A generation of NFL coaches and assistants, including Bill Parcells and Bill Walsh, were regular callers to his Globe cubicle.

Although McDonough was primarily a pro football writer, he also ventured into broadcasting, serving as an analyst for NBC and CBS.

On NBC's pre-game show, he sat next to O.J. Simpson. Will and his wife Denise were socially friendly with Simpson and his wife Nicole. Globe staffers say one of the few times McDonough was visibly shaken was when Simpson was charged with his wife's murder.

On the local Boston scene, McDonough was close friends with legendary Celtics coach Red Auerbach and often played handball with Auerbach. Although not a hockey fan, McDonough was also friendly with Bruins president Harry Sinden.

McDonough's columns were often stinging and harsh. He never pulled punches and he detested "phonies." He described Red Sox pitcher Roger Clemens as "the Texas con man."

When he took over a weekly notes column, his Saturday opinion piece was "must reading" not only for the general public but for all the movers and shakers in the sports world.

When McDonough spoke, people listened.

In 1981, the Massachusetts Interscholastic Association decided to move two Super Bowl football games from college sites to high school fields to save money.

However, the playing fields at those high school sites were badly chewed up during the Thanksgiving Day games, and many people were concerned that the athletes could be injured playing the Super Bowl games under unsafe conditions.

I had received a number of calls complaining of the use of the high school fields and began thinking about writing a column to recommend alternatives.

On the Monday morning before the Super Bowls, I was grousing at my desk about the field situation when McDonough decided to do something about it.

He picked up his phone and started talking. "Hello, Chuck (New England Patriots vice president Chuck Sullivan). This is Will. We're bringing a couple high school Super Bowl games down to Foxborough on Saturday."

A minute later, Will handed the phone to me. "Here, it's all set. This is Chuck Sullivan. You make the arrangements."

I told Sullivan it was very late to be making changes for the sites, but I would contact the MIAA and see what could be done. I contacted MIAA executive director Dick Neal, who spoke with Sullivan and agreed to change the games to the Patriots' home field.

It was a good thing that the changes were made because a snowstorm began that Saturday morning and the two games were able to be played at Foxborough. They would not have been played had they been scheduled for high school fields.

The tradition of playing the high school Super Bowls at the Patriots' home field, although interrupted occasionally, is still going strong with six games each year.

Without McDonough's phone call that Monday morning in 1981, it may never have been possible.

McDonough was involved in many charitable endeavors, but his greatest contribution was his idea to create the Red Auerbach Youth Foundation to honor his great friend.

Will came to me in 1983 with a request.

"We're starting a foundation to honor Red, and I'd like to have a couple of events run so people can see what we'll be doing in the future."

I arranged a freshman/sophomore track meet to be run by the Massachusetts State Track Coaches Association and a basketball clinic before a Celtics game. The track meet became a permanent part of the foundation and is run at the Reggie Lewis Track and Athletic Center in Boston.

A $500 a person gala was held in 1984, and the foundation was established a year later.

My involvement in the foundation continued after the initial fundraiser, as a member of the board of advisors. I served the foundation until I left Boston in 1994.

McDonough assisted me when I criticized his alma mater, Northeastern University, in March 1984.

My column was critical of Northeastern, which had purchased the Boston Arena in 1979 from the state for $250,000. Northeastern, which modernized the building, had agreed, as part of the sale, to allow Boston's high school hockey teams and for high school tournament games to continue to be played at the Arena.

However, I had received rumblings that Northeastern had not lived up to its agreement, and I argued that if it did not live up to its agreement, the state should compensate Northeastern for the Arena's upgrades and regain control of the facility.

A week after my column, Northeastern athletic director Irwin Cohen, a friend of mine, responded to my criticism with a piece in the Globe sports Sunday opinion page.

I wasn't sure of the outcome, particularly when I received a call from the college requesting me to attend a meeting with Northeastern University Vice President Jack Curry, who later became the college's president.

I was concerned about the meeting, and I didn't want to attend the meeting alone, so I asked McDonough if he would join me for the meeting. McDonough was a Northeastern classmate of Curry and was friendly with many members of the Northeastern athletic department.

McDonough accompanied me to the meeting, and to my relief, Northeastern agreed to make changes and to live up to its agreement.

McDonough was a great father and mentor to his sons. Sean McDonough has been one of the country's great broadcasters in a long and distinguished career. Terry McDonough is vice president of personnel for the Arizona Cardinals, and Ryan McDonough is general manager of the Phoenix Suns.

McDonough died of a heart attack in May 2003.

The magnitude of his impact on the Greater Boston community was such that his wake was held at the Fleet Center (the new Boston Garden).

Longtime friend and Boston businessman, Joe O'Donnell, quoted in The Globe's obituary on McDonough, said, "The characteristic about Willie I admired the most, over his tenure as a sports writer, then as sports celebrity, first regionally and then nationally, is he was a guy who could walk with kings, and he never forgot where he came from. I think of a guy who walks into NFL meetings and the commissioner greets him personally, and Willie's worried about the doorman getting the right tip. He never missed the common touch."

I talked with McDonough a couple of months before he died. "Willie, I've always wondered how you could criticize even the giants of the sports world, yet they spoke with you and often became friends."

"As long as you do your homework and write the truth, you'll always come out OK," he said.

McDonough was a mentor and friend to his colleagues, and I miss him greatly.

The Incredible Katie Lynch

When the phone rang at my Boston Globe sports desk in February 1992 little did I know I was about to learn about the most amazing person I would ever meet.

The caller was John Passarini, an adaptive physical teacher at Wayland High School.

I covered Passarini as a football, wrestling, and baseball standout at Newton South High. I followed his career at the University of Connecticut and I wrote about his starting the wrestling program at Waltham High.

Passarini said he believed he had a good story for our school sports pages.

"I have a student in my adaptive physical education class by the name of Katie Lynch. She is twenty-eight inches tall and was born with a form of dwarfism. She is manager of the indoor track team and was the wrestling manager last year."

He described Katie as a hard worker in his class and said her personality, despite her many physical disabilities, was sparkling.

I told Passarini I liked the idea and that I would assign one of my reporters to write the story.

"No, Larry, I want you to write the story," he responded.

There was silence at my end for a number of seconds. Normally, I would tell a coach that I won't tell him how to run his program and please don't tell me how to run my sports section. However, Passarini and I went a long way back and I respected his opinion. I agreed to do the story.

I'm glad he insisted because I would not have had a chance to meet and to know the most electrifying person in my life.

Katie Lynch was everything Passarini said she was—charming with a twinkle in her eyes, bright, and engaging. Despite all her physical challenges, she had an amazingly positive outlook on life and she was always smiling with a wonderful sense of humor.

Katie worked hard in Passarini's physical education class and considered herself an athlete. While most athletes worked hard to run, Katie trained hard just to be able to walk.

Her personal slogan was *Parva Sed Potens*, Latin for "Small but powerful."

My story on Katie ran atop The Globe sports pages on March 17, 1992. It was her introduction to the world. A week later, she appeared on "The Today Show."

A year later Katie graduated from Wayland High School and enrolled at Regis College in Weston. In May 2000, she graduated summa cum laude from Regis.

Katie was never far removed from Children's Hospital in Boston. She was a patient there for her whole life, undergoing more than a dozen life-threatening surgeries. She also worked at the hospital as a spokesman and became a sought-after motivational speaker.

Katie went from the national to international stage in April 2001. On the Saturday before the annual Boston Marathon, my former Globe colleague John Vellante wrote a Page One story on Katie's planned 26.2 foot marathon at the marathon starting line on Monday, the day of the marathon.

Katie underwent a rigorous training schedule to prepare for her personal marathon. Six times a week she underwent thirty minutes of water walking therapy and an exercise program.

Despite being in pain and not even sure she could complete the 26.2 feet, Katie was given medical clearance for the big event. She successfully navigated the marathon, and her accomplishment was chronicled with stories and photos in newspapers around the world.

I stayed in touch with Katie after we left Boston in 1994, and when my wife, Bunny, and I were in Boston in June 2002, we arranged to meet Katie at Children's Hospital in Boston. We spent a wonderful half hour with her before she took off in her motorized wheelchair for another appointment.

As we walked out of the hospital, I turned to my wife and said, "Spending a half hour with Katie Lynch is as uplifting an experience as anyone can have in life."

On October 24, 2002, Katie Lynch died at age twenty-seven, but my connection to Katie lived longer than her natural life.

Katie was buried in a family plot in Pennsylvania and a memorial service was scheduled for December at Regis College.

Joan Lynch, Katie's mom, enclosed a note in an invitation to attend Katie's memorial service. She wanted to make sure I was invited to attend the memorial service, but would understand if I couldn't attend.

That thought never crossed my mind.

In December, after finishing my night's work at The Ventura County Star, I drove to LAX and flew to Boston to attend the following evening's memorial service.

More than 700 attended the inspirational service at Regis College an hour and a half of of symphonic music and readings, followed by an hour and a half of speakers.

In my career as a newspaperman, I have attended a large number of funerals and memorial services, not none as inspirational as Katie Lynch's.

Dr. Frederick Mandell, who was Katie's personal physician her whole life, marveled how this young woman could handle all her medical challenges with as much grace and courage.

Passarini chronicled what is was like to be Katie's adaptive physical education teacher, and how hard she worked to achieve her athletic success. Passarini also marveled at Katie's warm but determined personality.

Edward Mulholland, director of continuing studies at Regis, admitted he was wrong to question Katie's acceptance at Regis.

"I felt college was no place for Katie," he remembered. "But Katie taught me more about life than anyone I've ever known."

I think of Katie often, and just the thought of her brings a huge smile to my face.

Katie's length of life was very short. But her accomplishments and her impact will live on for a very long time.

Katie's 185,000 To 1 Shot Comes Through

Katie Lynch was never a believer in odds.

At birth, she was only thirteen inches long and severely deformed. The diagnosis was of retardation and an early death.

Despite more than a dozen life-threatening operations and living in pain daily, Lynch became a bright, enlightened, and entertaining woman whose mere presence was enough to light up a room.

Her academic achievements at Wayland High School and Regis College were easily surpassed by her bubbly personality, the twinkle in her eyes, and her unwavering desire to battle overwhelming odds, no matter the challenge.

Katie's life changed dramatically the day she entered John Passarini's adaptive physical education class in eighth grade. Confined to a motorized wheelchair and needing around-the-clock care, Katie began her athletic career.

Her goal was simple—being able to walk a short distance.

Passarini worked feverishly with Katie over the years, and Katie, all 28 inches of her, trained with the same fervor.

Passarini never liked calling his students handicapped or disabled. "They are all differently-abled," he said.

In her senior year, Passarini worked with Katie for three months prior to her 1993 graduation. She shocked everyone by walking across the stage to accept her diploma.

On Patriots Day 2001, Katie competed in her own Boston Marathon, walking 26.2 feet at the start of the marathon in Hopkinton. Her walk was covered in stories and photos worldwide the next day. Katie died on October 24, 2002, but before she passed away, Katie, who valued Passarini's enormous dedication to his students, nominated him for the Disney Teacher of the Year Award in 2003.

Katie knew John was among thirty-six category finalists for the 2003 honor, an incredible accomplishment considering there were 185,000 applicants for the award.

In July 2003, Passarini and the other finalists gathered at Disneyland in Anaheim to be honored during a weeklong celebration that included seminars with all top teachers and a Disney parade in front of Sleeping Beauty's Castle.

Katie's mother, Joan, invited my wife, Bunny, and me to Disneyland for the celebration.

Passarini was selected as one of five finalists. Each of the finalists appeared on the nationally syndicated "Wayne Brady Show" the week before the final decision.

Passarini's show was taped on Thursday and was shown nationally on Friday. My wife and I joined Joan Lynch in the studio for the taping.

We were told that the winner was going to be announced on Brady's Monday show.

Somehow, we forgot to watch the show that morning. At 8 p.m., I remembered that we missed the show, but I wanted to know if Passarini had won.

I called Passarini's home in Lexington, Mass., despite the 11 o'clock hour, but there was no answer.

So I called Joan Lynch at her Wayland, Mass., home and apologized for calling so late.

"I wanted to know how John made out," I said to her.

"Would Katie have nominated anyone who wasn't going to be the Disney Teacher of the Year?" she said.

It was a classic response, but a wonderful way to tell me that Passarini, a 185,000 to 1 longshot for the prestigious award, had won.

Never Underestimate Doug Flutie

Throughout his extraordinary football career, Doug Flutie's talents were always questioned.

Way too short to be an effective quarterback was the frequent comment about the 5-foot, 9-inch Flutie.

Natick High football coach Tom Lamb was never in that position. Later, Boston College football coach Jack Bicknell was also an early Flutie fan.

Lamb found about Flutie very early in Flutie's sophomore year at Natick in 1978.

"We were in preseason, and we were having a coaches' meeting to discuss our most promising players," Lamb told me for a story I was writing for The Globe's 1984 Heisman Trophy special on Flutie on December 2.

"I asked the secondary coach about his top players. He mentioned a sophomore named Flutie. I reminded him that we had a policy of not starting, or even playing, sophomores," said Lamb.

"He's our best player," was the coach's response.

So Flutie was in the starting lineup for Natick's nonleague opener against Winchester.

In the second period, Winchester fullback Tom Murray, a Globe All-Scholastic the previous year, broke into the open and was one-on-one with Flutie, who tackled him, forced a fumble, recovered it, and rambled to the 15-yard line.

"We went on to score and won the game, 6-0," recalled Lamb.

Later in the season, Natick was leading Braintree 24-10 in the fourth period when Braintree scored 15 unanswered points.

Natick drove down the field but was faced with a fourth down situation.

Flutie came up to Lamb and asked if he could kick a field goal.

"Have you ever tried a field goal before?" Lamb asked.

"No," was Flutie's response.

For a reason unknown to Lamb even to this day, he allowed Flutie to try the field goal. It was good, and Natick won, 27-25.

Not that I disbelieved Lamb, but after our phone call, I went to The Globe's library and looked up the Natick-Braintree game on microfilm. There it was in the box score. N—Flutie 36 FG.

Flutie played quarterback and in the secondary for his junior and senior years, earning Globe All-Scholastic honors both years.

Natick was 7-3 in his senior year, "but we would have been lucky to be 3-7 without him," said Lamb.

Flutie was not highly recruited, and even schools that were interested in his services projected him as a defensive back.

Nationally, Flutie was not even among the Blue Chips recruiting service list of top players in America.

Boston College was among the colleges that wanted Flutie, but only in the secondary.

Flutie was chosen to play in the annual Shriners Football Game in June of his senior year at Natick. The game was being played at Boston College, where Flutie had been accepted.

"If I play well in the Shriners game, can I be added to the depth chart at quarterback? Flutie asked Bicknell. The coach agreed.

I had followed Flutie's career closely. His father, Richard, had written me a letter about his son when Flutie was a sophomore. "Please watch out for my son. He's going to be great."

I was a color commentator for the Shriners game on TV Ch. 56 in June 1981, and Flutie played impressively.

True to his word, Bicknell added Flutie to the quarterback depth chart, not that he expected his fourth string quarterback to see any action his freshman year.

Boston College, an independent, struggled in the early stages of the 1981 season, and was trailing traditional opponent Penn State 31-0 when Bicknell figured he had nothing to lose by seeing what Flutie could do.

Flutie passed for 135 yards and a touchdown in the game's final period. For the rest of his college career, Flutie was over center for every down for Boston College.

In Flutie's final regular season game, on November 23, 1984, he was pitted against highly rated Miami quarterback Bernie Kosar.

Boston College was trailing, 45-41, with six seconds left and BC at the Miami 48-yard line. Flutie went back to pass, rolled to his right, averted a tackle, and let loose with a pass that covered 64 yards in the air. His roommate, Gerard Phalen, was behind a trio of Miami defenders and caught the ball in the end zone as Boston College pulled out a miraculous

47-45 victory.

Flutie's pass is considered by many to be among the top individual plays in the history of college football, and the game ranks up there among the best games ever played.

Boston College was selected to play in the Cotton Bowl, BC's first appearance in a Bowl Game since the Sugar Bowl game against Tennessee in 1941. BC won the Cotton Bowl game, 45-31, over Houston.

For a player who was not considered to be a prized recruit, Flutie's career greatly impacted Boston College.

In the years following Flutie's graduation, applications to Boston College surged so much that it was called the Flutie Effect."

In 1985, Flutie signed a five-year, $5 million contract with Donald Trump's New Jersey Generals. The NFL's Los Angeles Rams still drafted Flutie as the 285th pick that year.

The fit was not good since the Generals' coach, Walt Michaels, was old school and didn't have a lot of confidence in Flutie and his style of football.

Interestingly, Bicknell was often asked why he didn't force the free-ranging Flutie to follow a certain offense. "I'd be foolish to ask a great talent like his to follow a certain regimen," said Bicknell.

Flutie was a pro football quarterback from 1985 to 2005. He played for nine different teams and was a successful starter in the NFL, but his greatest success came in the Canadian Football League, where he won three Grey Cup championships and was Most Valuable Player in each of his three title games.

Flutie threw for a record 6,619 yards for the British Columbia Lions in 1991 and had 48 touchdown passes for the Calgary Stampeders in 1994.

He played twice for his hometown New England Patriots, and on January 1, 2006, he made a dropkick, the first dropkick in the NFL since 1941.

Flutie is a member of the College Football Hall of Fame and the Canadian Football League Hall of Fame.

In retirement, he has been a broadcaster and color commentator for Notre Dame Football.

He also created the Doug Flutie Jr. Foundation in honor of his son, who has autism.

When people discuss Flutie even today, the first thing most often said is that he was too short to play football.

Hardly.

A Surprise Start For Flutie With Patriots

Anytime the Red Sox qualified for the playoffs, The Globe's coverage blew up.

So in 1988, when the American League championship series between the Red Sox and the Oakland A's opened at Fenway Park, Sports Editor Vince Doria sent the usual large contingent of reporters, columnists, and photographers to the game.

When the Red Sox qualified for the postseason, the paper usually ran two sports sections—an eight-page section for the playoffs and a four-page section to cover all the other sports news.

Game 1 of the ALCS was on Wednesday, October 5, the

same day that the Patriots conducted their midweek news conference in Foxborough. The midweek news conference gave the media a chance to get material for features and advance stories and to participate on a phone conference call with the coach of Sunday's opponent.

With most of the staff at Fenway, Doria called me into his office.

"We don't have anyone to cover the Patriots practice today. I'd like you to go down and do a short, basic notebook so we can have something on the Patriots in the paper," he said.

Occasionally filling in on a college or pro story was a nice break from my usual routine, so I went down to Foxborough for what I thought would be an easy, routine story.

I was very wrong.

Patriots coach Raymond Berry started the news conference by announcing that Natick's and Boston College's own Doug Flutie would be starting Sunday against the winless Green Bay Packers.

Since being acquired from the Chicago Bears in early 1987, Flutie started just once for the Patriots, guiding a 21-7 victory over Houston in a game involving replacement players a year ago.

Flutie was considered the No. 3 quarterback behind 14-year veteran Steve Grogan and backup quarterback Tom Ramsey.

Berry had sidelined Grogan, who had taken a beating in three straight games. Berry had replaced Ramsey the previous week when Flutie came off the bench to spark a 21-17 Patriot victory against the Indianapolis Colts, scoring the winning touchdown on a 13-yard bootleg with twenty-three seconds left. Subsequently, Flutie was named AFC offensive player of the week.

Asked why he was starting Flutie, Berry said," I just had a gut feeling."

When I returned to The Globe that afternoon, my "routine notebook" had changed from a small story on an inside page to a front page story of the sports section.

Flutie didn't fare well in his first start, losing, 45-3, to the Packers, but he led the Patriots to six victories in an eight-game stretch in 1988.

After playing for eight different teams in his professional football career, Flutie returned to the Patriots in 2005 as a backup.

In the Patriots' regular-season finale against the Miami Dolphins on January 1, 2006, Flutie successfully drop kicked a football for an extra point, something that had not been done in a regular-season NFL game since 1941.

It was Flutie's first kick attempt in the NFL and earned him that week's title of AFC Special Teams Player of the Week. Patriots head coach Bill Belichick, known for his knowledge of the history of the game, made comments that suggested that the play was a retirement present of sorts for his veteran quarterback.

'Subway Sam' Silverman

Sam Cohen, the venerable sports editor of Hearst's Boston newspaper, The Record-American, often boasted he was Boston's biggest promoter.

Because the paper's editions for the Record's newspapers came out at noon, 3 p.m., and 6 p.m., Cohen filled his sports pages with columns, stories, cartoons, and photos of boxing, pro wrestling, the Ice Capades, the circus, the rodeo, and press releases. Only the morning American carried results from baseball, basketball, hockey, and football.

Boxing was big in Boston. The Boston Garden was built as a boxing venue, and many big fights from the 1930s through the 1960s were fought in the Garden ring.

The biggest beneficiary of Cohen's largesse was Boston boxing promoter "Subway Sam" Silverman.

In advance of many big fights, Cohen ran stories on all the boxing cards in town, often with Bob Coyne cartoons and staff columnists accompanying the hoopla.

Many of the features and columns centered around Silverman, one of the most flamboyant figures in Boston sports history. Silverman had many nicknames. He was dubbed "Subway Sam" because he traveled the city's subways to drop of press releases and to conduct business at such venues as the Garden, Boston Arena, and Mechanics Hall.

According to Ring Magazine, Silverman also had the moniker of "Suitcase Sam" because he often kept a suitcase full of cash in the trunk of his Cadillac.

He also was called "Unsinkable Sam" because of his outsized personality during his nearly four-decade run as a promoter.

Controversy was the norm for Silverman. He often spent as much time in court as he did at a boxing venue. Reportedly, there were two attempts on his life, and the word was he often had his loyal wife, Helen, or some of his underlings, start his car outside his Chelsea home every morning.

But there was no doubt Silverman was a major player on the national boxing scene. He promoted more than 12,000 fights, including thirty-two of Rocky Marciano's forty-nine professional bouts.

When Sugar Ray Robinson was brought in to fight Paul Pender for a Boston Garden card, Silverman arranged with Robinson, one of boxing's greatest fighters, to train inside a store window at Raymond's Department Store in downtown Boston.

Reading as many as four or five newspapers a day growing up in the Dorchester section of Boston, I was well aware of Silverman and his flamboyant style.

So when interest in boxing declined, it was not surprising that Silverman had to move his fights to smaller venues.

In the mid-1970s, Silverman moved a lot of his fights to the North Shore, scheduling boxing cards at locations like the Golden Banana strip club in West Peabody and an ice skating rink in Danvers. When he first started promoting cards on the North Shore, I finally met Silverman when he dropped off one of his press releases to the sports office at *The Salem News*.

Silverman never recognized any sport other than boxing, and he often complained that boxing, particularly his fights, never received enough publicity. No matter how much coverage he received, it was never enough.

But Silverman had a charming side to him, and I admired his style. I covered a lot of his North Shore bouts. Very often the boxers and the bouts changed at the last minute, but I still enjoyed dealing with Silverman.

Salem News Sports Editor Bill Kipouras was also enamored of Silverman, and he felt a personal profile of Silverman would interest our readers.

So I prepared a feature story on Silverman, looking not only at the boxing promoter, but at the man, husband, father, and grandfather.

In early July 1977, my profile on Sam Silverman ran in *The Salem News.*

Silverman was overjoyed. He claimed it was the first story ever written about him that focused on his being a family man.

He stopped by the office a few days after the story ran to pick up extra copies of the feature. Wearing his traditional suit and smoking his usual cigar, he profusely thanked me for the story.

He then headed to Lowell, picked up a boxer, and drove to Albany, N.Y., for a bout that night.

Early the next morning, Silverman drove the boxer home to Lowell and then headed home to Chelsea.

He never made it.

At 6 a.m., on the morning of July 9, 1977, Sam Silverman suffered a fatal heart attack, crashing into a pole on Route 2 in Cambridge. He was sixty-four.

Joe Lazaro Never Let
Blindness Change His Life

In the spring of 1970, I was in the basement of Joe Lazaro's home in Waltham, Mass., attending a news conference for the first Joe Lazaro Blind Golf Tournament.

Lazaro, a national blind golf champion, was hosting the media to kick off what has become a well known annual tournament to benefit Lions Club charities.

A young reporter approached Joe and proclaimed, "It's nice to see you." He then cringed at the thought he might have said something inappropriate.

"It's nice to see you, too," said Lazaro, as everyone in the circle chuckled.

It was typical of Joe, who always made people feel comfortable around him.

Joe Lazaro could have easily felt cheated. Engaged to Edna Basnett, whom he met in England before being shipped to Italy during World War II, he was blinded by a land mine near Florence on September 9, 1944.

When he returned home, Lazaro offered to break off the engagement, but the future Mrs. Joe Lazaro refused, saying, "You're still the same person; you've just lost your sight." They were married in Waltham in April 1946.

Lazaro caddied at the Weston Golf Club as a teenager, but golf wasn't in his plans after he was blinded.

A close friend, Paul Fahey, changed that.

"I told Joe about blind golf," said Fahey, who explained that a caddie assisted a golfer by lining up the golfer with the ball and explained the layout of the hole, the length of the hole, and whether there were bunkers or water hazards. On the green, the caddie would explain the length of the putt and how the putt was expected to break.

Fahey said Lazaro was lukewarm to the idea originally, but eventually Fahey wore him down and Lazaro agreed to play.

Not only did Lazaro become a golfing legend, but he became a seven-time National Blind Golf champion and two-time International champion.

He was inducted into the first National Blind Golf championship Hall of Fame in the initial class in 2007, and he was named the 1980 New England PGA Man of the Year. In 1985, the National Blind Golf Association created an award for the most improved player each national championship. It is named the Lazaro Trophy.

His biggest golf honor was bestowed by the Golf Writers Association, who named Lazaro as the 1970 winner of the Ben Hogan Award.

Lazaro worked at Raytheon in Waltham and was more famous than Tom Phillips, the Raytheon president and CEO. Raytheon owned Amana, and Lazaro annually played in the Amana Open Pro-Am.

Reportedly, Lazaro challenged Arnold Palmer to a round of golf—with one condition—that they tee off at midnight.

When Lazaro was introduced to Tiger Woods in 2006, the PGA great said, "I know all about you."

Lazaro regularly shot in the 90s, but one year I received a weekly call from Wayland Golf Club, where Lazaro regularly played, indicating that Joe had shot a 77 that day. "That's not a net score—Joe actually shot a 77," the caller marveled.

It marked the first time a blind golfer had shot below 80.

Joe and Edna had three children and home life was unaffected by Joe's lack of sight — with one exception. Edna had to drive Joe around. "I guess you'll have to be my skipper," Joe said to Edna, and thus "Skip" became her nickname.

Joe mowed the lawn at night and tended to this garden.

When his children brought friends to the house, they often didn't realize Joe couldn't see because he didn't avoid normal chores around the house.

After more than sixty years of marriage, three children, four grandchildren, and a brilliant golf career, Lazaro, a man who enjoyed life and shared his joy with all he knew, died at ninety-five on Christmas Day in 2013.

Vargas Silences His Critics

Despite his 100-5 record as an amateur boxer and 14-0 record as a professional boxer, many in the boxing world wondered if Fernando Vargas was too young to be challenging IBF light middleweight champion Yori Boy Campas on December 12, 1998 at Trump's Taj Mahal in Atlantic City.

Two years before, as I became assistant sports editor at The Ventura County Star in Ventura, California, Vargas, from Oxnard, was the biggest story of the year.

Vargas had qualified for the 1996 Olympics in Atlanta, a year after winning a bronze medal at the Pan American Games. However, Vargas lost a controversial second-round decision in Atlanta. Despite the setback, Vargas turned professional and breezed to a 14-0 record.

Many boxing pundits questioned whether Vargas, only a week after his 21st birthday, should be challenging Campas in the nationally televised HBO fight. The biggest argument against Vargas taking the scheduled 12-round fight was his lack of experience, and that his longest fight had been six rounds.

Shortly after I arrived at the Trump Taj Mahal, I met with Lou Duva of Main Events, promoters of the fight. Duva had trained fourteen fighters who had won word titles and was well qualified to discuss Vargas' chances.

The purpose of my interview with Duva was two-fold. Aside from getting notes for my fight advance story, I was planning a what's next feature for Monday's paper if Vargas was victorious.

Duva had little doubt that Vargas was not only ready, but that he would dominate Campas.

Vargas wasn't the only one involved in his first world championship bout. In my thirty-three year journalist career, I had never covered a title match. I had covered Waltham boxer Donny Sennett in his fights at Waltham's IBEW Hall, and had followed Joe DeNucci's comeback, including a fight against Emile Griffith at Boston's Hynes Auditorium. I had also covered many of promoter Sam Silverman's cards on Boston's North Shore.

The only previous experience I had with a boxing champion was a Muhammad Ali news conference at a Boston restaurant, where Ali dazzled the media with his usual verbal repertoire.

Vargas was equal to the task on the big stage. He became the youngest IBF light middleweight champion by dominating Campas from the start and earning a seventh-round TKO victory.

The Oxnard boxer, also known by the nicknames Ferocious, the Aztec Warrior, and El Feroz, was on his way to the big time.

Vargas retained his title three times before he made his next biggest test. Vargas agreed to fight veteran Ike Quartey at the Mandalay Bay Events Center in Las Vegas on April 15, 2000.

Vegas had become the biggest boxing venue in the world, and a victory over Quartey would catapult Vargas into fights against the likes of Oscar De La Hoya, Felix Trinidad and Sugar Shane Mosley.

Las Vegas provided the glitz and glamour that no other venue could provide. Further, with Vargas' Mexican heritage, his fights drew large ratings on HBO.

Two days before the fight, there was a news conference at Caesar's Palace, complete with showgirls and other hoopla.

I had attempted to interview Vargas, but I was rebuffed a few times. I did manage a short "home town exclusive" interview after the news conference, riding with Vargas and his long-time trainer, Eduardo Garcia, in the limousine ride from Caesar's back to Mandalay Bay.

Worldwide celebrities attended the fight, including Mike Tyson, a friend of Vargas who came into Vargas' locker room to wish him well before the fight.

Speculation was that if Vargas won, a unification bout with Felix Trinidad would be in the offing. No less an authority than promoter Don King made that promise.

But Quartey was a tough opponent, entering the match with a 34-4-1 record.

Both fighters landed some heavy blows. Quartey's mouth and nose bled throughout the fight and his right eye was nearly closed in the late rounds when he couldn't see Vargas' hook.

Vargas once again silenced his critics with a sterling 12-round effort, connecting on 42 percent of his punches en route to a unanimous decision.

"Vargas stepped up," said King. "He was there to fight."

"People said I didn't have the experience, but as I always have, I showed them I was able to do the job," said Vargas.

Vargas retained his title in August 2000, scoring a fourth-round TKO over Ross Thompson in Las Vegas for his twentieth straight pro win, before meeting Felix Trinidad on December 2 in Las Vegas.

In his quest to reach superstar status, Vargas suffered a 12th-round TKO loss to Trinidad.

He lost to De La Hoya in 2002 and was beaten twice by Mosley in 2006, essentially ending his career.

Vargas was beloved by his fans, and he achieved much during his 26-5 career, but he didn't have the stuff to reach the highest levels of the sport.

Ed Schuyler, The Most Versatile Sportswriter In America

Most sports fans have a favorite beat writer or columnist. In most cases, he or she writes for a local paper or, in modern times, a national web site.

I was very fortunate to work at *The Boston Globe* with some of the best sportswriters and columnists in the country, but my favorite sportswriter was someone whose byline was generally overlooked and often omitted because he worked for The Associated Press wire service. Most readers overlook bylines and many newspapers ran AP wire stories by only crediting the wire service and not the writer.

I admired Ed Schuyler Jr., the New York-based AP writer who covered boxing and horse racing more than three decades. He started covering boxing for the AP in 1960, and I had followed his writing starting in 1965.

One advantage of working for newspapers was the ability to scan the Associated Press and United Press International wires.

Most of the AP writers specialized in one sport. Schuyler was an expert in two sports that might have been the most difficult to cover because the characters in both sports were significantly different from most other mainstream sports.

I liked Schuyler's style of writing, but his extensive knowledge of both sports and his obvious interviewing skills made his stories much more interesting to me. Whether I read an advance story, a feature, or match or race coverage, his writing was impressive.

Even more impressive was Schuyler's deadline skills. As soon as a boxing match or a horse race ended, Schuyler picked up his phone and dictated a short story to get the result on the wire. He followed with a quick story, and substituted both with a final story with quotes.

There were more famous boxing writers than Schuyler, but he covered more than 6,000 bouts and more than 300 world championship bouts in his thirty-five years on the boxing beat.

In 1979, he was presented the Nat Fleischer Award for boxing journalism excellence and was inducted into the International Boxing Hall of Fame in 2010.

Schuyler covered horse racing for the AP for thirty-nine years and was one of the most respected writers in the sport's history.

Because I was going to be on the east coast, I covered light middleweight boxer Fernando Vargas' first championship bout, for my paper, the *Ventura County Star.* It was Vargas's first IBF championship bout, against Yori Boy Campas, on December 4, 1998 at the Trump Taj Mahal in Atlantic City.

I called the AP in New York and asked if Schuyler was going to cover the Vargas-Campas fight. I was delighted to learn that he was going to be there.

I arrived in Atlantic City two days before the fight to prepare for a post-fight Monday morning feature if Vargas won the fight.

I met Schuyler in the press room before the Friday weigh-in. I enjoyed our discussion, his humor, and knowledge.

On Saturday night, Vargas, from Oxnard, Cal., knocked Campas out in the seventh round to earn the IBF junior middleweight championship. I filed two stories on the fight, the main story and a notebook.

On Sunday morning, I was heading to New York to visit with B.J. Schecter, who had worked with me at The Globe and had become an up-and-coming editor at Sports Illustrated.

I awakened early and went into the checkout line shortly after 7 on Sunday morning. While waiting my turn, Schuyler joined me.

He asked where I was going, and I told him I was driving to New York.

"I'm taking a bus back to New York. Would you mind driving me to the bus station?" he asked.

"I'd be happy to," I said. We checked out while my rental car was being brought by the valet.

Schuyler said he didn't know where the new bus station was, but he knew the general area. After driving around for a few minutes, I turned to Schuyler and said, "Look, I'm heading to New York. I can drop you off at the Port Authority bus terminal."

He agreed, and we headed to New York. What a joy it was for me. The long ride seemed to take little time because Schuyler filled the ride with his life story and the incredible number of great boxers and horses he had covered.

It was a wonderful experience. I had the opportunity to meet and get to know someone I had admired for a long time.

Bob McIntyre Cleared All The Hurdles Of Life

Of all the people I worked with on the high school level over a four-decade career in sports journalism, no one could compare to Bob McIntyre, whose stamp on high school sports in Massachusetts was as great as anyone who ever lived.

Mac, as he was known to all, was a quiet giant, always tirelessly working on behalf of the youth of Massachusetts. He never took credit for anything, but he was always plugging away to make everything better.

He was an outstanding cross country, track, and football coach at Andover and Melrose high schools, but his mark was made on a higher level.

When the West Newton Armory was demolished in 1958, McIntyre began the battle to find another location for the high school track meets. He never stopped waging the fight, and he lived long enough to see the building of the Reggie Lewis Track and Athletic Center.

He was president of the Massachusetts Coaches Association in the late 1960s when The Globe's Marvin Pave and The Herald's Bill Abramson came up with the idea of high school Super Bowls for football. Mac loved the idea and helped make the Super Bowls a reality.

Mac was the most organized person I ever met. He and Weymouth North track coach Dudley O'Leary knew how to run cross country and track meets better than anyone.

When Mac and O'Leary conducted meets, they ran with amazing efficiency.

I remember one time when the New England track meet at Providence ran hours late, and we couldn't get the story and results in for the first edition of the Sunday Globe. When my reporter called me on deadline to tell me it would be a while before the meet even ended, my reaction was, "This wouldn't be happening if Mac were running this meet."

Ironically, the best work of his life came in his last decade when he battled cancer.

In November 1989, McIntyre was fighting lymphoma, and he appeared to be failing fast. On Christmas Eve, doctors told the family death could be in a matter of minutes or hours.

O'Leary was at Mac's bedside and pleaded with his family to pull the plug and let him die because the pain was so excruciating. But Mac was a fighter. He not only survived the night, but overcame cancer a second time before succumbing to the disease on November 1, 1997 at the age of seventy-two.

In the eight years he lived after his initial cancer diagnosis, Mac always said, "I awaken every day appreciative of the opportunity to be alive."

Over the eleven years I wrote about building the track, McIntyre was the foot soldier, lobbying at the legislature and keeping the drive going.

When Globe colleague Will McDonough started the Red Auerbach Youth Foundation, he wanted to find an event that could show donors the kind of work the foundation would be doing.

I called McIntyre, who suggested a freshman-sophomore track meet that would help developing track standouts in a major meet setting.

The experimental Red Auerbach Youth Foundation Freshman-Sophomore Meet is still being run, a testament to the genius of McIntyre.

Mac was also a counselor and friend to all. When I had written a column critical of Massachusetts Interscholastic Athletic Association Executive Director Dick Neal, I received a call from McIntyre.

"I agree with the position you took in your column this morning, but you were too harsh. You have to realize that while people may be wrong about an issue, they really, deep down, believe in their position," he said.

From that day on, every time I wrote a critical column, Mac's words resonated with me.

Mac never believed the track would be built. "I'll believe it when they hand me the keys," he joked. And, in 1995, he was handed the keys.

The Reggie Lewis Track and Athletic Center is the culmination of Bob McIntyre's dreams. And, despite never wanting or taking credit for his yeoman work, the track is named in his honor, a fitting tribute to a man whose hard work and dedication made a huge difference.

A Coaching Legend Into His Mid-80s

When Lexington football coach Bill Tighe concluded his football coaching career with a 14-0 victory over Burlington on Thanksgiving Day 2010, I knew it would be impossible to speak with him for a while.

The Massachusetts legend was concluding 60 years of coaching and had favorably impacted the lives of thousands of young men in six decades.

I waited for a few weeks to try and call Tighe, then 86. When I did start calling, all I got was busy signals.

When my wife and I were in San Francisco for a few days in late January, we were in a shopping mall when I decided to try once again.

To my surprise, Tighe answered.

"I'd have an easier time speaking with the Pope than I've had trying to speak with you," I said.

Tighe's response was his legendary chuckle.

A classy and modest man, Tighe always has had a positive approach to the daily challenges of life and a simple philosophy.

"I always look beyond," he said.

Tighe based his views on a lifetime of triumphs and tragedies. Tighe and his wife, Mary, had six children, but two had Cystic Fibrosis. Billy died when he was thirteen and Michael was among the oldest living Cystic Fibrosis patients in the world when he died in his late thirties.

In 1988, Tighe had to deal with another crisis when he had rectal cancer. He underwent a colostomy and fully recovered.

"I feel lucky," said Tighe at the time. "This is the biggest win of my life and I've been given a clean bill of health. I remember going to Children's Hospital when the boys were younger and seeing so many other children with problems much worse than ours."

When he retired, Tighe was the oldest high school football coach in the nation.

Tighe grew up in Ashland. He played football, basketball, and baseball at Ashland High, graduating in 1942 and heading directly into the Army.

He served in the Army Air Corps in the southwest Pacific as a warrant officer and crew chief for the P38s.

After World War II, he enrolled at Boston University and played under Buff Donelli. In the days of two-platoon football, he was a quarterback and safety. In 1948, his senior year, a freshman named Harry Agganis enrolled at BU. "It was lucky for me that freshmen weren't eligible then," kidded Tighe, who had a close relationship with Lynn's Golden Greek.

Tighe became a teacher-coach at Wakefield and was an assistant football coach under Jim Walsh in 1949. He remained an assistant until he was elevated to head coach in 1957. He moved over to Malden in 1964 and coached there until 1972. In 1975, he took over at Lexington, turning around one of the most unsuccessful Division 1 programs.

Tighe, who was president of the Massachusetts Football Coaches Association in 1969-70, was the longtime chairman of the association's Hall of Fame Committee. During the 1984 inductions, Tighe was a surprise recipient.

The executive committee had voted him in even though it was customary to induct retired coaches.

Lou Racca, a former Wakefield school committee member and a longtime Tighe assistant coach, hailed Tighe when he was inducted by his colleagues.

"Bill is one of the finest men I've ever known. He was a guidance counselor even before there were guidance counselors," said Racca.

"I love football because it is the only sport I know of that teaches young men to have complete control of themselves, to gain self-respect, give forth a tremendous effort and, at the same time, learn to observe the rules of the game, regard the rights of others and stay within the bounds dictated by decency and sportsmanship," he told me for a story in 1988.

"It has been an honor for me to have played a small part in the lives of these beautiful young men who taught me and inspired me to strive day by day to be worthy of the title coach, a precious trust given by God to mold and shape our country's No. 1 resource—the lives of our young who will be tomorrow's leaders."

"Bill Tighe is the most beloved sports figure in the history of Lexington High sports," said John Conceison, a Worcester Telegram and Gazette sports copy editor and a graduate of Lexington High.

His fellow coaches were huge admirers of Tighe.

"Bill is one of the nicest men I've ever met, a true gentleman. Bill was a great competitor on game day," said former Woburn coach Rocky Nelson. "He changed with the times and motivated and got along with kids."

Former Melrose coach Bruce MacPherson said Tighe was the most respected of any guy in the state. "Bill's a wonderful guy who was a great credit to the profession. As much as anyone, Bill was responsible for the status of high school football in Massachusetts. There was a charisma about him."

Tighe believes his success can be attributed to "my love of people. I love all people and can get along with everyone. I love music and have played banjo all my life. I love having a sing-along."

Tighe, now ninety-three, enjoys spending time with his children—Sharon, Maureen, Kevin and Steven—and six grandchildren.

The Courage, Perseverance Of Vic 'El Gato' Ortiz

Minutes before Vic Ortiz was scheduled to undergo a kidney and liver transplant at Boston's Beth Israel Hospital on October 16, 2008, a member of the surgical team came out of the operating room and spoke with Ortiz's wife, JoAnn.

"You can stop the surgery now," said the doctor. "There's no way he's coming out of this alive."

JoAnn Ortiz refused to halt the surgery. Doctors had told her that her husband had less than forty-eight hours to live, and she insisted the surgery go forward.

After an eight-hour double transplant, Ortiz emerged from the surgery.

Nine years later, despite many setbacks and many medical scares and procedures, Ortiz is still going strong.

Ortiz had previously dealt with heart issues, major back surgery, and a serious blood infection. He has subsequently endured heart valve and hip replacements and a stroke. His new kidney lasted five years and he is on a waiting list for a new one. He is sustained by dialysis three times a week.

Vic Ortiz was one of my favorite high school coaches. He coached Brockton High's basketball team from 1983 to 2007, guiding the Boxers to 386 victories, five sectional championships and one state title (1995). He has been inducted into the Brockton Hall of Fame and the Massachusetts and New England Basketball Coaches' Halls of Fame.

Ortiz was also an adjustment counselor and a teacher in Brockton for thirty-one years. His role as a counselor helped steer many students in the right direction, a major feat since Brockton High had more than 5,000 students. The school was, at one time, the second largest high school east of the Mississippi.

He was a no-nonsense coach, a strict disciplinarian. But at the same time, he was fair and his players respected him because he cared for them so much.

Ortiz achieved his success despite not having a single 1,000-point career scorer.

A native of Indiana who grew up in Puerto Rico, Ortiz fought for his players.

When the Massachusetts Interscholastic Athletic Association refused to grant senior Curtis Bostic a waiver for his senior season in 1989-90, Ortiz and Brockton went to bat for him.

Bostic had turned nineteen before September and was ruled ineligible by the MIAA.

Ortiz and Brockton requested a waiver for Bostic, whose mother was killed right in front of him as an eighth-grader. Bostic missed much of that school year and had to repeat the eighth grade. As a result of repeating the eighth grade, Bostic had passed the eligibility age of nineteen before the start of the school year.

Given the circumstances that caused Bostic to repeat the eighth grade, the MIAA's refusal to give Bostic a waiver, rankled a lot of people, including me.

I wrote a column supporting a waiver for Bostic, joining a large chorus of voices opposing the MIAA's actions. The MIAA opposed the waiver request for more than five months and in two courtrooms. Only when Plymouth Superior Court Judge Cortland Mathers remanded the case back to the MIAA just before the start of the season in December, did the MIAA finally relent and grant Bostic a waiver.

Had the MIAA not done so, Mathers had scheduled a 9 a.m. appointment for the next day, when he vowed to order the waiver.

Bostic's stellar play at Brockton earned him an opportunity to play at the University of Cincinnati, where he is now the strength and conditioning coach.

Ortiz and I had been friendly before the Bostic case, but my support for Bostic took the friendship to a different level. Vic and JoAnn were guests at our family's Passover Seder, and my wife, Bunny, and I were privileged to enjoy a spectacular paella dinner prepared by Vic at the Ortiz home in Brockton.

Even though we are separated by 3,000 miles, Ortiz and I stay connected by phone on a regular basis, and when my wife and I return to Boston, we have enjoyed our reunions with the Ortizes.

Despite his many medical challenges, Ortiz has remained a fervent believer in his Catholic faith and greets every day with his appreciation of life.

I have nicknamed him El Gato, Spanish for The Cat, for he is still working on his Nine Lives.

Bob Walsh Was A Statistical Wizard

Over a decade and a half of supervising the school sports section at The Globe, I made a lot of changes and discoveries.

My greatest discovery was Bob Walsh, who never scored a touchdown or kicked a field goal. And he wasn't a coach. He was a statistical wizard whose passion for history made him one of the most important high school football figures in Eastern Massachusetts.

Walsh, who died in 1998 at age seventy-nine, helped brighten the high school sports pages of The Globe for nearly two decades. His enthusiasm and vast statistical knowledge of high school football helped produce charts, graphs, and stories that made The Globe's scholastic football coverage that much better.

In an era of sloppy record-keeping, Walsh stood out. He chronicled each Eastern Massachusetts football result in a hard-bound notebook for more than six decades.

He devoted the entire second-floor den of his Saugus home to high school football records, and his basement was full of Boston and North Shore newspapers dating to the 1930s.

Walsh's acumen was chronicled in a full-page feature in The Globe in 1980, and shortly thereafter he began contributing stories and statistical charts. Walsh worked for months preparing material for The Globe's pre-Thanksgiving coverage.

Walsh spent more than 1,000 hours researching every facet of interscholastic football from 1888 through the 1979 season—from the exploits of legendary coach Bill Broderick to every imaginable team record and statistic.

"From the time I was a little kid, I loved anything old," said Walsh. "I remember one summer in Nantasket that I found some old records in my grandmother's attic. I've always had an interest in ancient things."

Walsh first researched the history of football in the North Shore. That project culminated in a 1979 four-part series in the Daily Evening Item of Lynn. But once he started, Walsh could not stop with just the North Shore.

"The project started small and just grew. I've always been intrigued by the uniqueness of Eastern Mass. football. It's so ancient, predating all other kinds of football in the United States —college and professional," said Walsh.

Walsh went to the Boston Public Library and spent days looking up statistics. He enlisted the help of school football buffs such as Ernie Young of Haverhill, John Boy of Everett, Waltham sports editor Frank Murphy, Harry Lojko of Salem, George Richards of Malden, John Thomas of Ipswich, and Lexington football coach Bill Tighe.

No statistical stone was left unturned by Walsh. His statistical wizardry has resulted in a portfolio that included such categories as Eastern Mass. champions from 1888-1979, the best 50-year records, schools with the most titles, records of longest winning streaks, most undefeated seasons, longest on-going winning streaks, a look back at the oldest Thanksgiving series, and the best coaching records of all Eastern Mass. Hall of Fame inductees.

When a local player had a standout performance, a call inevitably was made to Walsh, who cheerfully researched the request and called back with information that helped put the accomplishment in perspective.

A talented artist, Walsh also occasionally contributed cartoons to the school pages. A newspaper reporter, artist, and government information officer, Walsh was delighted when The Globe first published one of his cartoons. Having one of his cartoons appear in The Globe was a lifelong dream.

In the early 1980s, when The Globe revived the Bus, a cartoon feature honoring unbeaten football teams that first appeared in the paper in 1938, Walsh helped prepare information about Gene Mack, The Globe cartoonist who drew the Bus from 1938 until his death in 1952.

Walsh obtained an original Mack cartoon, which helped younger Globe readers understand the background of the cartoon.

Walsh's writing style was folksy, and his tales of years gone by brought the past to life.

Because of his exposure in The Globe, Walsh received requests for information from all across New England. He never turned anyone down.

In a discussion I had with Walsh about high school baseball, I mentioned that there were no records available about the state high school baseball tournament.

Over the next several months, he researched the tournament history, poring over microfilm at the Boston Public Library. He spent hundreds of hours putting together material that resulted in a full-page Globe feature and, naturally, included every championship result.

In my entire career, I never met anyone who had more passion than Bob Walsh.

Our readers were the beneficiaries of that passion.

SECTION TWO
THE EXPERIENCES

My Week With The Boston Bruins

Before heading to The Globe office on Sunday, January 17, 1982, I decided to dress warmly and casually.

Being a weekend day, I didn't have to wear a shirt and tie, and with the temperature at two below zero, I put on a flannel shirt and dungarees, and layered with a ski parka, ski hat, scarf, and gloves.

My wife, Bunny, packed a brown bag dinner since the Globe cafeteria was closed on Sundays.

I arrived at the office at 1 p.m. and dropped by assistant sports editor Ron Indrisano's desk. Indrisano was the editor in charge of the sports department that night.

"How's it going, Ronnie?" I asked. I received a grunt in return.

So I headed to my desk to set up my day's work, which was preparation of the two weekly high school pages which ran on Tuesday.

Once settled, I stopped by Indrisano's desk and asked my question again.

"We have a problem," said Indrisano. "Frannie (Rosa, The Globe's Boston Bruins beat writer) has a bad back and can't make it to Philly tonight for the Flyers' game, and Marantz (Steve, the backup Bruins' beat man) can't go because his wife, Alison, is due tomorrow.

"I've tried to get Al Morganti (a former Globe intern when he was in college in Boston), and see if he can send us his (Philadelphia) Inquirer game story, but I haven't been able to reach him."

"We can't use a Philadelphia game story in our paper," I responded. "I'll go to Philly and cover the game."

"Just do the game story and don't worry about a notebook," Indrisano advised.

I called U.S. Air and booked the 3:30 flight to Philadelphia and then headed to Logan Airport.

The flight was delayed because the plane had to be de-iced, but we finally took off and arrived in Philadelphia shortly after 6. I ran into Channel 7 sports anchor John Dennis after I deplaned, and we took a taxi together to the Spectrum.

We arrived at the Spectrum, and after I picked up Rosa's credentials at the press gate, I found my way to the press box just minutes before the opening faceoff.

"What are you doing here?" was my greeting from Bruins public relations director Nate Greenberg, a longtime friend from our part-time days at *The Boston Herald* in the mid-1960s.

It would not be the last time I was to be so greeted that night. I explained the circumstances to Greenberg and sat down to cover the game.

I read the pregame press notes and noticed that the Bruins had released veteran NHL forward Dick Redmond, who hadn't registered a single point in a number of games with the Bruins.

Despite Indrisano's request to avoid writing the notebook, I knew we couldn't leave the big news out of the paper. I wrote a brief notebook, filed the story, and called Indrisano to tell him to add the notebook to the Bruins' jump page.

By writing the notebook, I had to rush and catch up with the running game story. Because of early deadlines for the paper's first edition, beat writers chronicle the game by period, then put on a lead with the final score.

The Flyers handed the Bruins a 7-3 drubbing.

After filing the first edition story, I went down to the Bruins' locker room to get quotes.

When Bruins coach Gerry Cheevers saw me, I was greeted by the familiar, "What are you doing here?"

I had covered Cheevers and the Bruins when I worked at *The Salem News*, and his son, Craig, who was a senior hockey played at North Andover High, had been featured in a Globe school sports page story.

With quotes from Cheevers, Bruins and Flyers players, I returned to the press box and wrote and filed my updated game story. Exhausted by my long day, I was ready to get some sleep. I asked the Flyers' beat writers if someone would be kind enough to drive me to the Sheraton Hotel at the airport.

One of the writers obliged.

Close to midnight, I checked into the Sheraton, picking up Rosa's reservation. I opened the door to my hotel room, only to be greeted by a blast of cold air.

It was below zero in Philadelphia that night, and the maid had shut the heat off when she made up the room earlier that day. I turned the heat on, but the room was still cold all night.

I called Delta Airlines and booked the 7 a.m. flight back to Boston.

While watching *North Dallas Forty* on TV, I dined sumptuously on my brown bag dinner that my wife had packed for me more than twelve hours earlier.

I made a 5 a.m. wakeup call and then fell asleep.

When the phone awakened me after a four-hour slumber, it was time to go to work.

I didn't have a razor and blades or toothpaste and toothbrush, so I took a hot shower, got back into my not-so-nifty clothes and headed downstairs for the 6 a.m. shuttle to the airport. As I entered the shuttle, I was greeted by Bruins' vice-president Tom Johnson, one of the NHL's great defensemen who played for the Montreal Canadiens.

En route to Boston, I smelled smoke in the cabin, but my fears were allayed when a flight attendant announced that breakfast had burned in the microwaves.

When we arrived in Boston, I picked up my car at the airport and headed to the Globe office to start my work day. I needed to edit all the school sports pages' copy and prepare a layout to be made up in the composing room.

Shortly after 10, Sports Editor Vince Doria arrived in the sports department.

"I see you were in Philly last night," he said nonchalantly as he glided by my desk.

At 4:30, I was ready to go home and relax after my one-day adventure with the Bruins.

Not so fast.

Doria called me into his office and told me I was going to Pittsburgh in the morning.

"Frannie's still not ready, and Alison hasn't given birth yet," he said. "So, you'll be covering the Bruins' game Wednesday night in Pittsburgh."

I called my wife and asked her to pack my bags for a three-day trip to Pittsburgh.

I also said that we wouldn't be going to our son's elementary school that night for a poetry reading program.

I headed to Pittsburgh the next morning, covered the Bruins' practice, and wrote an advance for the Wednesday game before having dinner with some of the Bruins' beat writers.

The Bruins played much better against the Penguins, but still lost, 5-4, making my record covering the team a dismal 0-2.

The next morning, I flew home, expecting that my time covering the Bruins was over.

Marantz covered the Bruins on Thursday night at home, and Boston beat the Toronto Maple Leafs, 4-2. Marantz was also at the Boston Garden on Saturday night when the Bruins beat the Washington Capitals, 3-1.

I was preparing to go home Monday night at 5:30 when Doria told me Alison was in labor and that I would be returning to the Garden to cover the Bruins' game against the Atlanta Flames in a couple of hours.

The Bruins peppered Atlanta goalie Reggie Lemelin with 55 shots that night, but were lucky to escape with a 3-3 tie on a Ray Bourque goal with eight minutes left in the game.

In the Bruins' locker room, Greenberg kiddingly told me I was no longer welcome since I had posted an 0-2-1 record covering the team.

After a hectic week with the Bruins, I was ready to go back to my normal schedule.

Paul Mooney, Larry Moulter, And The Building Of The New Boston Garden

I'd never met Paul Mooney, president of the Boston Garden and the Boston Bruins, when I wrote a column about him in The Globe on March 26, 1986.

Mooney came to Boston in 1975 after Delaware North purchased the Boston Bruins, Boston Garden, and Channel 38 in Boston for the minuscule price of $10 million a year earlier.

Mooney's father, J. D. Mooney, the winning jockey aboard Black Gold in the 1924 Kentucky Derby, was a friend of Delaware North founder Louis Jacobs. Reportedly, Jacobs had told his son, now Delaware North chairman Jeremy Jacobs, that Paul Mooney was to be "taken care of."

Mooney was an irascible individual. Combined with Delaware North's reputation for thriftiness, Mooney created tremendous disdain for both himself and Delaware North.

Many of my Boston Globe colleagues had written critical pieces condemning Mooney.

My column attacked Mooney for reducing the number of high school events in the Garden.

A request to bring back the Eastern Mass. basketball sectional finals to the Garden in 1986 was met with a cold shoulder. Certainly, future pro Rumeal Robinson and Cambridge Rindge & Latin would have packed the Garden that year.

The Massachusetts Interscholastic Athletic Association had been trying to negotiate a new agreement for rental of the Garden for five years. Requests to meet with Mooney were continually met with no response. Each year, the old arrangements were renewed when tourney time rolled around.

The Garden had been taking 65 percent of the gate for the first $35,000 and 55 percent of the gate thereafter. The MIAA wanted to change the figures but couldn't get together with Mooney.

Mooney further showed his lack of class by ordering the press box closed for the 1986 state hockey championships. While the public might not have been interested in how inconvenienced the fourth estate might have been, I wrote that Mooney's action was an embarrassment to his employer.

I raised the issue of Mooney because Delaware North Corp. wanted to build a new arena.

However, I wrote that Mooney had done little to endear himself to the local clientele.

He brought down the Bruins' popularity by negotiating radio contracts that made it almost impossible to listen to the Bruins games in Greater Boston.

His relationship with the labor force at Boston Garden was notoriously poor. Some of his blowups with the media and others made many people wonder why Delaware North would want someone so embarrassing to be in such a prominent position.

Building anything in Boston, as in many cities, is almost an impossible task. Building a new arena would be even harder. Any developer would need to be a solid citizen and have an impeccable image.

And, certainly, if Delaware North were in the picture, elected officials would be wary if Paul Mooney was to stay around.

My column on Mooney had run on Easter Sunday. It was scheduled to appear the previous Sunday, but the high school column was not a priority, and it had been held because of space. I was at the office the evening the column appeared, and at 8 o'clock, I received a call from a member of the Garden bull gang (the crew that shifted the Celtics' basketball court to the Bruins' hockey rink).

"You made our Easter," the caller told me.

I wasn't surprised at the reaction.

The following March the boom was lowered on Mooney, who was replaced as Boston Garden president by Larry Moulter.

My only reaction was that I was glad that Mooney was gone.

A couple of weeks later I received a call from a Michael Goldman. "I know who you are," I told Goldman, a well-known Democratic political consultant.

"Your column was the reason Paul Mooney was fired," Goldman said.

"So many others had criticized Mooney. Why my column?" I asked Goldman.

"Your column was the straw that broke the camel's back," he responded.

Moulter, a political operative and literary agent, was hired with the goal of repairing the damage Mooney had done in his twelve years at the Garden. The secondary goal was building a new arena.

Moulter immediately "set up" shop at a restaurant in the Bostonian Hotel, a short walk from the Garden and Quincy Market.

He held breakfast, lunch, and dinner meetings with all the major financial, political, sports, and media players in the city and the state.

Several months later, I was summoned to the Bostonian for a breakfast meeting.

"Why me?" I asked Moulter.

He told me part of his responsibility as Boston Garden president was to improve Delaware North's image in the community.

He wanted my help to create what he called a "Good Sports" program, which honored high school athletes who achieved beyond the playing field.

Once established, the program's honorees were recognized annually—one year in between periods of a Bruins game and the next year at halftime of a Celtics game.

I also served as chairman of the selection committee.

At the initial breakfast meeting, Moulter told me one of his goals was to bring the Grateful Dead band back to the Garden.

The Grateful Dead was among the most successful musical groups ever. Their concerts sold out within hours, and the dates at the Garden were very profitable.

Mooney, it seemed, was irritated at the band members because, during one of their visits, some of the band members were cooking lobsters on a hibachi perched on one of the fire escapes at the rear of the Garden building.

Mooney ordered them off the fire escape.

The Grateful Dead vowed never to return to the Garden, but Moulter eventually convinced them to return to the Garden, one of his many successes.

Moulter worked day and night to achieve his goal of building a new Garden.

He organized a sixty-year birthday party for Boston Garden in 1989. It was one of the grandest parties ever held in the city. Invitees included all the greats who had ever graced the Garden, including Celtics, Bruins, boxers, pro wrestlers, Ice Capades performers, rodeo stars, etc.

Political heavyweights, the financial community, and other bigwigs were also there, as were all the Boston Garden employees. The food was top shelf, including a massive cart of shrimp with the largest shrimp you could ever imagine.

The evening's entertainment was a Boston Symphony Orchestra concert, reportedly at a cost of $100,000 for the evening. Moulter, the image of Delaware North significantly improved, weaved his magic on the political front.

And in a few short years Moulter accomplished the impossible. He built the new Boston Garden, to be known as the Fleet Center, which opened in 1995.

My wife, Bunny, and I were invited to attend the final night of The Boston Garden and the opening night of the Fleet Center.

It was the completion of one of the most unusual rides in Boston sports history.

The State Track
Thirty-Eight-Year Odyssey Finally Ends

High school extracurricular activities, particularly sports, were hit hard after Massachusetts voters passed tax-cutting Proposition 2 1/2 in 1980.

Several programs were drastically cut, and user fees were introduced all over the state.

Months after the proposition took effect in 1981, Boston Superintendent of Schools Robert Spillane announced a plan to eliminate all high school sports in the city.

It was at that point that I began my advocacy on behalf of high school athletes in Boston.

I was a 1962 graduate of Dorchester High School in the city. Although I was living in suburban Peabody, I always believed, and even more so today, that everyone should remember where he/she came from.

America is an immigrant country, and over the centuries, most immigrants entered the country and lived in urban areas, often living in poverty and working harder to achieve the American dream.

Unfortunately, many people who have left the city and prospered have forgotten their roots.

I was going to make sure that would not happen to me.

I wrote a column in The Globe condemning the superintendent's decision to eliminate high school sports and successfully helped rally opposition to the superintendent's plan.

Twice I successfully argued against elimination of the athletic director's position and I attacked Boston Mayor Ray Flynn for the decline of Boston high school sports during his tenure.

Flynn, who had played basketball at South Boston High and Providence College, was the biggest beneficiary of Boston sports, but while vocally supporting school sports in Boston, he did little to improve the programs.

I'm not sure of the exact day in 1982 that I decided I would begin to wage a battle to get the state track facility built.

Nor did I ever realize that the effort would take eleven years and have more ups and downs than a roller coaster.

Indoor track athletes ran their big meets at the West Newton Street Armory in Boston, but the building was in the path of the Mass. Turnpike extension project. In 1958, the building was demolished.

Efforts began immediately to build a replacement.

In 1964, a bill passed the legislature calling for a track at Cleveland Circle in the Brighton section of Boston. However, the NIMBY (not in my back yard) factor killed that effort.

Fast forward to 1975 when Governor Michael Dukakis signed into law a bill which called for a track in the Neponset section of Dorchester. That effort died when House Ways and Means chairman Tom Finnegan blocked the bid for the track, which would have been built in his district. Hard to believe that a single legislator could be so powerful, but there would be further setbacks precipitated by single legislators and one governor.

My involvement in the quest to build a new state track began in 1982 when I wrote a column, "It's Time to Build the Track." Over the next decade, I wrote more than 100 columns or news stories about the track. On the weekly high school pages, I ran a "Track Watch" brief, outlining the days it had been since a track bill originally passed the legislature.

It wasn't until 1987 that Dukakis filed a bill to build a $35 million athletic facility on the campus of Northeastern University. The facility would be utilized by the university, but would include a track facility for high school track.

In the final hour of the legislative session, at 12:44 a.m. on January 5, the legislature approved $35 million for the facility.

In 1988, the legislature approved construction by the turnkey method, the first of its kind in state history.

The debate over the turnkey method and the selection of the contractor pushed the start of construction into 1991 when Dukakis left office and Bill Weld became governor.

This delay resulted in another setback in the quest for a new state track facility.

According to many sources, Weld was not interested in building the track and providing a legacy for Dukakis. Weld was angry at Dukakis because, during the 1990 governor's race between Weld and Boston University president John Silber, Weld had asked Dukakis not to begin construction of a jail at New Braintree. Weld opposed building the new jail, but Dukakis rejected his plea and began construction anyway.

In June 1991, six months into Weld's governorship, there had been no action taken to move the Northeastern facility forward.

I called Weld's chief of staff, Steve Tocco, and made an appointment to see him at the state house.

Our meeting was very short but not very sweet.

"The governor has no intention of building the track," Tocco told me, and offered no explanation. I left the meeting extremely dejected.

The following week I ran a full-page feature announcing the death of the state track facility. The latest bid for a track had started in 1987, and was killed in 1991, and I vowed not to enter the fray unless I was given an opening.

The irony is that Rodney King was primarily responsible for the track finally being built.

In April 1992, Los Angeles was rocked by widespread rioting, looting, and acts of arson after four white policemen were acquitted of nearly all assault charges in the videotaped beating of King, a black motorist who was subdued under a barrage of police batons.

There were riots in urban areas across the country, but the black community in Boston's Roxbury, Dorchester, and Mattapan communities remained calm.

Weld came to Roxbury to thank the minority community for not rioting.

In his remarks, Weld said, "I promise you social and economic opportunity."

As I read Weld's comments in the next morning's Globe, I turned to my wife, smiling, and said, "We're back in the ball game!"

Weld had given me the opening for which I was hoping.

Over the next few weeks, I stepped up the pressure.

I wrote, "OK, governor, if you promised social and economic opportunity, I have an idea for you."

My renewed blitz was not viewed favorably within the walls of The Globe. Sports Editor Don Skwar criticized me for writing two columns on the track in one week.

Over the years, others in the sports department said I looked foolish writing about the track. After all, they had argued, bigger and better names had tried to get the track built. How was I going to succeed when no one else had been successful in more than thirty years?

Despite the opposition of my colleagues, I pushed forward.

In May, I received a call from House Speaker Charlie Flaherty (D-Cambridge). "I spoke to the governor and told him there would be no budget without a track bill," Flaherty told me. Flaherty and Weld filed a bill to authorize a $17 million track at Roxbury Community College.

In July, the House of Representatives voted overwhelmingly to approve the bill.

However, the track was blindsided days later when another single legislator, albeit an extremely powerful one, applied a knockout punch.

On the day the State Senate was scheduled to vote on the bill, I called Globe State House Bureau Chief Frank Phillips. I fully expected the Senate to pass the bill, and I requested that Phillips call the sports department with the vote. "We'll write a brief for the morning paper and I'll follow that the next day with a column," I told Phillips.

Shortly after 7 that night, I arrived home. Moments later, the phone rang. "The Senate killed the track bill," was the information passed along.

Fuming, I put my coat back on and drove to the State House. I tracked down one of the senators, and I asked how this could this happen.

After all, this was a bill filed by the Democratic speaker of the house and the Republican governor.

The senator told me, "When the bill came up for a vote, Bulger (State Senate President Billy Bulger) walked out of the chambers. That's the signal to vote against the bill.

"Bulger was miffed because he wasn't asked by the speaker and the governor to join them in the filing of the bill."

I drove home, as despondent as I ever had been.

When the State House opened the next morning, I headed to the Senate clerk's office and requested the roll call on the track bill. When I reached the office, I was shocked at how many senators who came from strong track areas had voted against the bill.

My column that Sunday was the most scathing of my career.

I attacked Bulger (D-South Boston) for his bizarre opposition to the bill. How, I wondered, could a Boston legislator, kill a bill that benefited the youth of Boston?

I questioned why the governor didn't make sure the Republicans in the senate voted for the bill.

I criticized all the senators who came from strong track communities and reminded their constituents to remember how their senator had voted on the track bill.

I singled out Sen. Walter Boverini, (D-Lynn), who had always boasted he had done more for high school sports than anyone in the state. Boverini voted "present" on the bill.

Next to my column I ran the roll call vote, perhaps the first time a Senate roll call had been published in The Globe sports section.

The column ran on the following Sunday, followed the next morning by an editorial criticizing the killing of the bill.

On Tuesday morning at 11 a.m., my phone rang. "Hi, Larry, this is Charlie Flaherty. "The Senate, on a voice vote, passed the track bill this morning, and it's on its way to the governor's desk."

Flabbergasted, I asked Flaherty, how it was possible for the bill to be voted on again. "Once a bill is killed, it can't come up for consideration until someone files a bill in the next legislature."

"Senate counsel (Joseph Brady) ruled last week's vote was unconstitutional, so the voice vote was taken," Flaherty said.

I told Flaherty that while I was glad that it appeared that there were no more obstacles to getting the track built, I was appalled at the process.

State Track Coaches Association executive director Bob McIntyre remained skeptical. "I'll believe we have a track when I'm handed the keys to the building," he always said.

McIntyre was correct to be wary. "We've climbed the 1,000 steps needed so many times and then we always tumbled back to the bottom," he said.

McIntyre was almost correct one final time.

Weld signed the bill, but before it could proceed, four pubic hearings were held.

The morning after the fourth hearing was held, McIntyre called me. "Twenty minutes before the hearing ended, (State Sen.) Dianne Wilkerson came in and asked that traffic and environmental impact studies must be done," McIntyre told me.

I called Wilkerson at the State House to verify her appearance at the hearing.

I asked her if she were aware that traffic and environmental impact studies had already been made. I further questioned why a Boston state senator would try to derail a building designed for Boston youth.

Wilkerson responded by hanging up on me.

On the following Sunday my final column on the track was a plea to the Legislative Black Caucus to silence Wilkerson.

Two days later a member of the Legislative Black Caucus called to tell me Wilkerson had been directed to back off.

In 1993, I attended the groundbreaking for what would become the Reggie Lewis Track and Athletic Center. On that day, I officially ended The Track Watch at 10,852 days.

The track was completed in the summer of 1995, and on November 5, 1995, the opening ceremony was held.

There were several ironies in the last push for the track:

Weld, the only governor to openly oppose building the track, was the governor who built the track. The building is the best indoor track in America.

Bulger left the Senate presidency to become president of the University of Massachusetts, but he resigned on August 7,

2003 for failing to aid a federal investigation of his mobster brother, the infamous James "Whitey" Bulger.

Wilkerson was sentenced to house arrest in December 1997 after pleading guilty to failing to pay $51,000 in federal income taxes in the early 1990s. She was suspended from practicing law for one year in 1999 because of the conviction and did not seek reinstatement.

In 2001, she was fined $1,000 by the State Ethics Commission for failing to report properly that a bank she lobbied for as senator was paying her more than $20,000 a year as a consultant. In September 2005, the state Attorney General and head of the state's campaign finance office filed a lawsuit against Wilkerson, alleging she had not reported nearly $27,000 in donations and refused to explain more than $18,000 in personal reimbursements. She agreed to pay a $10,000 fine and forego about $30,000 in debts owed her to settle the allegations.

The state Office of the Bar Counsel filed a complaint on October 3, 2008, accusing Wilkerson of violating the rules of professional conduct. It argued Wilkerson lied under oath at a 2005 court hearing at which her nephew, Jermaine Berry, requested a new trial on a manslaughter conviction.

On October 28, 2008, Wilkerson was arrested by the FBI on public corruption charges. A federal criminal complaint was filed against her that alleges she was caught on tape stuffing a cash bribe into her bra and accepted those cash payments in exchange for her official duties and responsibilities.

Wilkerson was the subject of an eighteen-month-long undercover investigation conducted by The Boston Police

Department and the FBI in which she allegedly accepted eight bribes in cash totaling $23,500.

The bribes were allegedly accepted in return for her help in obtaining a liquor license for a proposed nightclub and transferring public land to a federal agent posing as a private developer.

On November 18, 2008, a federal grand jury indicted Wilkerson on eight counts of accepting bribes.

On January 6, 2011, Wilkerson was sentenced to three-and-a-half years in prison for bribery.

Chronology Of The Reggie Lewis Track And Athletic Center

1958: Discussions begin for new high school track facility.

1962: Governor Endicott Peabody signs appropriation for indoor track facility.

1964: Bill No 395 passes House of Representatives calling for a school track facility to be built at Cleveland Circle.

1965: Judge denies injunction barring start of construction of track facility at Cleveland Circle.

1966: Boston architectural firm says $1.3 million school track facility will be ready by 1968. It will be dedicated as the John A. Ryder Memorial Track named in honor of the late Boston College track coach.

1970: Bill instructing MDC to build $3 million track facility passes both branches of legislature and is sent to Gov. Francis Sargent.

1972: MDC agrees to construct track at Neponset site.

1974: House of Representatives in capital outlay budget, approves $2.3 million for purchase of land at Neponset. It also approves $3,987,000 for school track. facility, park and recreational facilities, bicycle paths and boat and canoe launchings.

1974: Gov. Sargent, calling his announcement "a victory night for the young people of Boston." Says construction of track facility will begin in March 1975.

1975: On December 30, MDC announces plans for massive athletic complex at Neponset Gov. Michael Dukakis says, "I remember the debate on this way back in the early 1960s. It was needed then and it's needed now and I'm delighted that after all these years were finally going to be able to go ahead with it."

1976: Unless there is an additional $1.4 million the school track project could be in danger of falling through.

1977: Many area residents back Neponset site for track. Rev. Msgr. Gerard Shea says complex will provide "something worthwhile for the young people to get out and exercise instead of standing around drinking." However, Neponset residents drop objections to facility because the are promised new MDC hockey rink.

1978: Rep. John Finnegan of Dorchester plans to go to court to block construction of $7.4 million track accusing Dukakis of "breaking faith" with the legislature and the community by directing the legislature to go ahead with the track project.

1979: Finnegan, chairman of Ways and Means Committee, introduces amendment which strikes school track facility from Neponset site. The amendment is approved.

1980: Finnegan begins discussions with Northeastern University. With state aid the university could build a facility which would house the track facility.

1983: Northeastern students vote more than 9-1 margin to pay student activities fee which would help build athletic complex on campus. Certain objections by Boston Redevelopment Authority and MRTA stall project.

1985: Interest in track revived, with state Reps, Joe DeNucd and Kevin Fitzgerald spearheading the drive at the State House.

1987: Gov. Dukakis announces plans for track on Columbus Avenue.

1987: In November, Gov. Dukakis files construction bill for track.

1988: On January 5, sixteen minutes before final session of Legislature, $35 million is appropriated for facility.

1988: On July 16, Legislature approves construction of the project by the turnkey method.

1990: On April 4, project goes out for bid and draws six development teams.

1991: Agreement with Northeastern is finalized but Gov. William Weld indicates he will not authorize construction of track at Northeastern.

1992: Gov. Weld and Speaker of the House Charles Flaherty file bill for $17 million track at Roxbury Community College. Bill passes House and Senate by July and Weld signs it into law.

1992: Mayor Flynn and BRA director Paul Barrett sell city

parcel, located at New Dudley and Tremont Streets, to state. In December, BRA votes to hand over parcel to the state.

1993: Groundbreaking.

1995: Track completed in summer. Opening ceremony on November 5.

1995: The first meet is December 23.

The 1990 AP Sports Editors Convention

When Globe Assistant Managing Editor/Sports Vince Doria left in 1989 to join the executive staff at the fledgling *National,* his successor, Don Skwar, inherited what he viewed as a giant headache.

Doria had been extremely active in the Associated Press Sports Editors Association and was instrumental in getting The Globe to be the host for the 1990 Associated Press Sports Editors Convention.

Skwar was one of the great idea editors of his time and was an incredibly hard worker who was as organized as anyone could be when it came to details dealing with the sports section.

As for other matters, such as minutia, his focus wasn't as strong.

As Skwar planned the difficult task of organizing the June convention, he brought his assistant sports editors into a meeting.

"I know one thing for certain," he said to us, "I hated the way they registered for the 1989 convention in Portland (Oregon). There were long lines, and it took forever to register. I don't want that to happen to us."

He tasked me with the registration process, and that's how I started my unofficial role as operations manager of the convention. As the convention neared, my number of jobs kept rising.

The convention ran from Wednesday, June 27 to Saturday, June 30. There were seminars and workshops on Thursday morning through Saturday morning, three sponsored meals a day, culminated by the annual awards dinner.

The Globe's commitment for the convention was $30,000, not including the rooms needed for Skwar and Assistant Sports Editors Bill Griffith, Robin Romano, and me at the Westin Boston, the host hotel.

There was much work to do. Aside from finding editors to serve on panels for the workshops and seminars, a program book was needed to be prepared, and special events such as a Red Sox game at Fenway Park and the Saturday softball tournament needed to be organized. Griffith and Romano worked ferociously for months in preparation for the convention.

The Globe had built a reputation as one of the best sports sections in the country, and the paper wanted to make sure the convention would enhance its image nationally.

As reservations poured in, it was obvious that the convention would likely break a record for attendance. There was a record 220 sports editors, not including wives and children. Overall, there were more than 400 people there.

My job began Monday morning, June 25, when I went to The Globe cashier and received $300 in petty cash for gratuities, and I picked up a company vehicle to have on hand. I had arranged for 250 souvenir bean pots from our promotion department as part of the packet each editor received at registration.

On the Monday morning before the convention, we met with the Westin staff, including five department heads. At the conclusion of the meeting, I handed each department head a

$20 gratuity. The two bell captains received two tickets each to a Red Sox game.

On Monday night, my wife, Bunny, and I put together 250 registration packets, including the bean pots, programs, and other tourist and Boston area information. My wife had gone to work in neighboring Brookline that morning and after work came to the Westin, where we stayed for six days.

The convention began on Wednesday afternoon. I had hired five former Globe co-op students to handle the registration, and we organized the registration alphabetically.

Thankfully, the process went smoothly, which addressed one of Skwar's biggest concerns. The social part of the convention was a nightly hospitality suite, which stayed open until 1 a.m.

Starting on Thursday morning, my work day at the convention was 4 a.m. to 1 a.m. At 4 a.m. Thursday, I awakened and headed to the front entrance of the hotel to greet a Globe truck, which dropped off 250 papers each day.

Prior to the convention, I had run off the daily schedules, and when the papers were delivered, I stapled the daily schedule to each paper. The hotel staff then delivered the Globe to each of the 220 rooms.

We had specifically requested that circulation deliver the paper's fourth edition, which would have all the West Coast results included in the sports section. That would prove to be a major boost for the paper's reputation with the delivery of the Saturday paper.

As the convention began, I walked around the convention floors to make sure everything went smoothly. When a problem arose, I called the proper department and received quick attention. My tips were either $5 or $10, depending on the task, and word spread quickly among the staff. Throughout the entire convention, the service was fast and impeccable.

The social highlight of the convention was the Friday night game between the Red Sox and Rangers. There was great anticipation in the months leading up to the convention that a Roger Clemens vs. Nolan Ryan matchup would happen. Many of the sports editors had indicated that the opportunity to see beloved Fenway Park was part of the reason they were attending the convention.

We had hired three trolleys to ferry the sports editors and their families to the game, and at 5:30 that night, we began loading the trolleys.

Unfortunately, neither Clemens nor Ryan pitched that night. One sports editor, Bob Kennedy of the Stamford (Conn.) Advocate, was anticipating the game because Stamford native and Rangers Manager Bobby Valentine was on hand that night. Kennedy was a close friend of Valentine, but joy turned to sorrow when Valentine was ejected in the first inning.

During the game, it was posted on the Fenway scoreboard that Dave Stewart of the Oakland A's had pitched a no-hitter. Glenn Schwarz, sports editor of the San Francisco Examiner, saw the posting and tracked me down.

"I need to make a call and tell the staff how I want this story handled," he told me.

I took him up to the press box, and he called the Examiner sports department.

Midway through the game, it started pouring, and it didn't stop. As the clock reached 10 p.m., the game had not been called off, but I started gathering the sports editors, telling them that the game was going to be called off and we had to start returning to the trolleys.

I had no idea if the game was going to resume, but I did know that at 11 p.m., the trolley overtime charges would begin, and the cost of the evening would escalate greatly.

We were able to get everyone back before 11, and from the hospitality suite we were able to see that the game had resumed. At 1 a.m. when the hospitality suite closed, the game was still going on.

Late that night, Fernando Valenzuela pitched a no-hitter for the Dodgers against the Cardinals, marking the first time in modern major league history that two no-hitters were pitched on the same day.

The Globe copy desk, recognizing the enormity of the record, changed the front page of the fourth edition that night to highlight the twin no-hitters.

When the sports editors saw our coverage in their delivered Saturday morning papers, there were kudos passed along for getting the news into the paper in such a prominent spot, even late at night.

On Saturday morning, the editors had a run from the hotel to the Charles River and back. As the runners were preparing to start, I felt something was missing. We hadn't provided water, so I called for bottled water, and a case of Evian was quickly dispatched.

I drove along the route to make sure everyone was safe and had additional water.

The awards ceremony on Saturday night was a fitting conclusion to a wonderful convention. Dave Smith, who had hired me at The Globe in 1978, received the Red Smith Award for lifetime achievement.

The convention ended Sunday morning when everyone checked out, but I was exhausted. I told Skwar I was staying an extra night, and he agreed.

The hotel was grateful to The Globe staff for assisting their effort, and we each received one free night at any Westin worldwide.

When the hotel manager found out that my wife and I were staying an extra day, he offered us a limousine for the day.

That afternoon, we had the limousine drop us off at Quincy Market, where we spent a good part of the afternoon. We called the limousine driver when we wanted to go back to the hotel, and we had a wonderful dinner and went to bed.

On Monday morning, I checked out and returned to The Globe. I filled out my weekly expense sheet, which included the entry $300 in gratuities.

I stayed by my phone that morning, fully expecting a call from the cashier's office wanting an explanation for the $300 expense that didn't include any receipts.

I wasn't disappointed. In late morning, the call came from Head Cashier Maureen O'Brien questioning the expense.

"It was the best $300 we ever spent," I told her, and left it at that.

Saving The Sports Editors' Softball Tournament

One of my many duties as an assistant sports editor at *The Boston Globe* was fixing problems. One of the lessons I learned as a young reporter was never to give up when working on a story. That persona carried over to include not giving up on any endeavor.

When The Globe hosted the 1990 Associated Press Sports Editors Convention at the Westin Hotel in Boston, my assignment was to make sure everything related to the convention went smoothly.

A couple of hours before trolleys full of sports editors were to head to Fenway Park to see the Boston Red Sox play the Texas Rangers on a Friday night, we were informed by the Boston Parks and Recreation Department that the two softball fields we had reserved for Saturday at the Boston Common had been reduced to a single field. A neighborhood group had requested use of the field, and a neighborhood group trumped The Globe on the priority list.

The annual softball tournament was held on the Saturday afternoon before the closing dinner and awards ceremony.

Four teams, representing four regional areas, competed. The winners of Game 1 advanced to the second game and the championship of the two-game tournament.

I knew we would not be able to overturn the ruling, so I tried to come up with an alternative. I called Boston Parks and Recreation Department Commissioner Larry Dwyer to come up with a solution. However, I was unable to reach him.

Knowing I needed to find fields, I called my friend Larry McIntire of the Salem Recreation Department. "I would be happy to help you out, but all our fields are being used on Saturday," McIntire told me.

Next on my list was longtime friend Russ Halloran, head of the Newton Recreation Department. There was no answer, and I left a message for Halloran to call me later that night.

At that point it was time to load the Fenway-bound trolleys for the Red Sox game.

When we returned to the Westin late at night, Halloran returned my call. "If you need our fields at Albemarle (in Newtonvillle), they are yours," said Halloran, who called back despite dealing with a heart attack suffered by his mother that day.

I went to bed that night knowing I had secured fields, but I would still need to acquire some transportation to the Newton fields.

Early the next morning, I was able to reach Dwyer.

"I really don't want to know what happened and why the field was taken away," I told Dwyer. "We need two fields and a bus to get us there. We have sports editors from papers like the *New York Times, Chicago Tribune, Miami Herald, Washington Post, and Los Angeles Times,* and they expect to be playing softball this afternoon. If we can't play the games, this is not going to look good for Ray (Boston Mayor Ray Flynn)."

Dwyer promised to call me back in a half hour.

True to his word, Dwyer called back. "We have two fields for you in South Boston. And there'll be a bus to take you there and bring you back. You'll be welcomed by one of our park supervisors."

I called Halloran and thanked him for his help, but told him that Boston had come through for us.

Three hours later, at 12:30 p.m., my wife, Bunny, and I escorted the bus to the South Boston softball fields, where a park crew was chalking the two fields.

A park supervisor greeted us. "Here are your two fields. We have a Boston Police officer to protect the sports editors, and we have a Police Athletic League trailer that will provide a barbecue for you."

Under sunny skies and warm temperatures, the two-game tournament was an athletic and social success.

'Berrying' The Super Bowl

During the 1950s, when there was no NFL team in Boston, the New York Giants were our home team on TV. We also viewed other teams' games on national television.

When the Baltimore Colts' games were on, I always enjoyed watching the passing combination of Johnny Unitas and Raymond Berry.

That admiration for Berry changed to disdain when he became coach of the New England Patriots and knocked a high school Super Bowl game out of Sullivan Stadium in 1986.

Berry scheduled a walk-through practice for Sullivan Stadium on December 6, a day before the Patriots' game with the Cincinnati Bengals.

Berry's move, announced in the spring, essentially eliminated the Division 3 Super Bowl game out of the stadium.

Thanks to Globe colleague Will McDonough, high school super bowls started to be played in Foxborough in 1982. They had become a welcomed and appreciated gesture from the Patriots.

Berry said he wanted the practice on artificial surface because, unlike AFC East rival teams, whom the Patriots play twice each season, the Patriots played the Bengals only once. He felt the team's regular field was better suited for the practice than the team's grass practice field a mile away from the stadium.

Berry met with the Massachusetts Interscholastic Athletic Association in late May to discuss the problem.

He agreed to terminate the walk-through practice by 10 a.m., which would allow the first of three games to be started at 11 a.m. That compromise wouldn't work, according to MIAA Executive Director Dick Neal.

I was baffled by Berry's insistence on conducing the walk-through practice on Sullivan Stadium turf. I checked with McDonough and many other NFL sources, and they described the walk-through practices as nothing more than roll calls. One source told me that the early-morning practices were held to make sure the players had not partied or worse on Friday night. I was furious that the Patriots did not realize the public relations disaster their coach had created, but they didn't want to interfere with his coaching decisions, and they chose to suffer the PR hit.

I wrote a column critical of the decision. My main criticism was that by allowing Berry, an outsider, to make a decision that was harmful to high school sports, the Patriots were guilty of lessening the value of high school sports.

What amazed me even more was the fact that Berry's father, Raymond, had been the high school football coach in Paris, Texas, for more than thirty years, and his background should have made him more sensitive to high school concerns.

I further argued that had Berry been coach of the Dallas Cowboys and had pulled a championship football game from the Cowboys' stadium, there would have been serious ramifications.

As effective as I believed my column to be, a Larry Johnson cartoon accompanying my column was the real crusher.

Johnson's cartoon showed Sullivan Stadium in the background and Berry, shovel in hand, digging up a grave with a marker showing the words "Berrying the Bowl."

My anger on this issue multiplied when the Massachusetts State Football Coaches Association supported Berry's decision, claiming as a coach he had the right to decide where practices should be conducted.

I attended a meeting of the coaches' association in October at Bentley College to discuss its position.

"I am appalled at your decision to support Berry," I told the coaches. "Massachusetts football is much weaker than most other states'. You weaken it even more when you allow an outsider to come in and do something that harms high school football."

My stay at the meeting lasted two minutes. I finished what I had to say and walked out. As a result of the walk-through practice, the Division 3 Super Bowl in 1986 between Lincoln-Sudbury and Lynnfield was moved to Boston University.

Fortunately for Berry and the Patriots, Foxborough barely missed qualifying for the second spot in the Super Bowl. Had Foxborough been one of the two teams in the Super Bowl, the Patriots, who needed much municipal help from the town of Foxborough, would have been an even more gigantic public relations disaster for the Patriots.

Berry had won Round 1 in this battle, but there would be another day and another battle to wage.

There was no issue in 1987 because the Patriots were on the road the weekend of the high school Super Bowl. But the Patriots and their coach created another public relations nightmare a year later when Berry scheduled a walk-through practice the day before they played the Seattle Seahawks at Sullivan Stadium.

Once again, I wrote a column critical of Berry and the Patriots, this time two months before the high school Super Bowls.

"High school sports takes a back seat in this part of the country because people have always been willing to accept what people in power have thrown at them. As long as the high school community and the fans sit back and accept the status quo, interscholastic sports in Massachusetts will be second rate," I wrote.

On national election day 1988, when George H. W. Bush was elected president, I was at the Nikko Hotel in Chicago at a meeting of the Gatorade Circle of Champions national advisors. I received a call at the hotel from the Globe sports department that Berry had relented and agreed to move his walk through practice from Sullivan Stadium.

The high school Super Bowls have become a great tradition at the Patriots' home field, particularly with Bob Kraft as owner of the team.

Berry was wrong to make his stand, and I was pleased he ended up not getting his way more than once.

A Baseball Trip Is A Bonding Experience

My son, David, and I had been talking about doing a baseball trip for some time, and in 1992, when he was seventeen, we decided to do it.

Working long hours and even longer weeks as an assistant sports editor at The Globe, I felt I had cheated my son of valuable hours and days with me. The baseball trip was an ideal bonding time.

Ironically, in July 2014, the baseball experience, albeit a single game between the Baltimore Orioles and the New York Yankees at Camden Yards, extended to another generation when I took my grandsons Kaden and Vance to the ballpark.

I took a picture of the two boys behind home plate with the entire field behind them. Recalling the 1992 baseball trip, I checked my memorabilia from that trip and found a Globe travel story I had written in September 1992.

With the story, The Globe had run a photo of my son that I had shot. Ironically, it was taken in almost the exact spot where I had taken the pictures of my grandsons.

In an otherwise rainy summer, the baseball gods were with us on the eleven day, thirteen game, 2,200-mile trip.

We did not have a drop of rain on the highway, nor was any game rained out. A shower in Canton, Ohio, and two rain delays in Baltimore one night were the only inconveniences we encountered. We were also fortunate that we didn't run into any traffic jams or highway accidents and, amazingly to my son, we didn't get lost.

Bobby Valentine, the former Rangers' manager, was a recurring part of our baseball vacation. We had seen Valentine and the Rangers lose to the Toronto Blue Jays, 3-2, in Arlington, Texas, the week before we started our baseball trek from Boston on June 29. Valentine and the Rangers were 3-2 victims once again when we visited the SkyDome in Toronto on July 1.

And when we concluded our trip, staying our final night in Stamford, Conn., following a Yankees-Mariners game at Yankee Stadium, the next morning's Stamford Advocate offered three stories on the firing of hometown hero Valentine by the Rangers the day before.

The trip blended the charm of Class A, AA and AAA baseball in Auburn, N.Y., London, Ont., and Canton, Ohio, with the tradition of Tiger Stadium, Cleveland's Municipal Stadium and Yankee Stadium, and the excitement of the newer parks such as the giant, $500 million Toronto SkyDome and Baltimore's terrific Oriole Park at Camden Yards.

Unlike at stoic Fenway, fans at other parks reveled in fast-paced organ and piped-in music. We joined in the traditional 7th-inning singing of "Take Me Out to the Ballgame." Giveaways ranged from fast-food meals to accounts at the local bank. Baseball was only part of the attraction.

We were in Toronto on Canada Day, their version of our Independence Day, and we saw military stuntmen descend to the ground on ropes from the huge CN Tower and fireworks inside the closed dome following Toronto's victory. The SkyDome was closed, then reopened to remove the smoke following the fireworks. In Canton, we saw fireworks, and skydivers landed on second base in a pregame feature.

Esso towels and Canadian flags were among the presents for fans in Toronto. Commemorative pins were handed out in Detroit and Cleveland.

There were touches of home along the way. In Auburn, N.Y., we renewed acquaintances with former Malden High three-sport star Carmine Cappuccio, The Globe's first Male Athlete of the Year. He had recently graduated from Rollins College and was beginning his professional baseball career with the Utica Blue Sox.

In Cleveland, Paul Sorrento, a former Globe All-Scholastic via St. John's Prep, didn't disappoint fans from his hometown of Peabody, by hitting a home run in a 6-1 Indians' victory over the Oakland A's.

There were plenty of baseball highlights during 117 innings and 132 runs in thirteen games. During a doubleheader at Tiger Stadium, we witnessed a rare triple play and Lou Whitaker's 200th career home run.

The Yankees managed six runs in the first inning on a single hit against Seattle. And we did get our share of stolen bases.

Our most ambitious day was July 4. After watching the Tigers and Mariners split a five hour, thirty-minute double-header in Detroit the night before, we headed for Cleveland early the next morning, arriving one and a half hours before the day game. No sooner had the Indians dispatched the A's than we were on our way to Canton, where we saw the Reading Phillies prevail, 5-4, that night.

The next day, the public address announcer at Thurman Munson Memorial Stadium in Canton, urged patrons to turn to page 26 in the program. "If there's a Canton-Akron Indians stamp there, you win two free tickets to General Cinema," he advised.

I dutifully checked page twenty-six, and turned up a winner. The two tickets sealed the evening's activity. After watching the Class AA Indians topple the Reading Phillies, 9-7, we headed to the movies to watch, naturally, "A League of Their Own," the summer's smash hit about the women's professional baseball league during World War II.

The trip wasn't all baseball, though. By leaving early each morning for the next destination and scheduling venues only three hours apart, we were able to see sights in each of the cities before arriving at the park at night.

We visited the Hockey Hall of Fame in Toronto and the Pro Football Hall of Fame in Canton, home to the McKinley Memorial, a tribute to the late president. En route from Buffalo to Toronto, we stopped and gazed at the beauty of Niagara Falls. My son, a lacrosse player, didn't want to miss the Lacrosse Hall of Fame, adjacent to Johns Hopkins University's fabled Homewood Field on its beautiful Baltimore campus.

We bypassed the Baseball Hall of Fame in Cooperstown, N.Y., because it had been included on an earlier trip that featured visits to three Halls of Fame—baseball, basketball, and soccer.

Our favorite locale was Baltimore. Fortunately, we had planned to spend two days there, and it was worth the extra time.

Oriole Park at Camden Yards is located on the edge of downtown Baltimore on the site of former rail yards. The park's designers built a modern stadium with the past in mind, and the structure blends beautifully with its surroundings. A rehabilitated warehouse behind right field is all that remains from the original site.

Babe Ruth's birthplace in a brick house a few blocks from the new home of the Orioles also houses the Orioles Hall of Fame. Along with Maryland crabs, it's a can't-miss attraction. Local legend has it that the Babe's father operated a bar where center field at Camden Yards is now located.

The Inner Harbor, its fine shops and restaurants and the aquarium, a favorite of my son, made the visit to Baltimore complete.

The baseball highlight in Baltimore was a stolen base by former Red Sox catcher Carlton Fisk. Baltimore catcher Jeff Tackett was so stunned, he didn't even bother to throw to second base to get the sliding 44-year-old Fisk, then playing for the White Sox.

As we headed home the morning after the Mariners-Yankees game, my son and I talked enthusiastically about our adventure.

"Maybe we can fly into Chicago next year..." he said.

Our son, now forty-two, and I agree that our baseball trip was the best time we ever spent together.

High School Football Was My Family On Thanksgiving

Thanksgiving in America is family, turkey, cranberry sauce, pumpkin pie, and football.

For most of my life, Thanksgiving was high school football.

As a second generation American descended from Eastern European immigrants, Thanksgiving was not a big holiday when I was growing up in Boston in the 1940s. Even when we did celebrate the holiday, turkey wasn't on the menu.

When I became a sportswriter at *The News-Tribune* in Waltham, the holiday began my association with high school football, which has been played in Massachusetts on Thanksgiving since the 1880s. The holiday games usually featured the teams' top rivals.

From 1965 to 1993, I spent most of my Thanksgivings involved with covering games and eventually piecing together eight pages of Thanksgiving football coverage.

My most memorable Thanksgiving Day as a writer came in 1971 when a blizzard hit Massachusetts. I was scheduled to cover the Newton North-Brookline game, but that game and almost the entire slate of eighty-plus games were postponed to Saturday because of the blizzard.

News-Tribune Sports Editor Frank Murphy called me at home and told me there was one game in our area still scheduled—Our Lady's of Newton against St. Columbkille's of Brighton—and that I would be covering it.

Unlike most high school football stadiums, there was no press box at the field in the Nonantum section of Newton, meaning I would have to cover the game on the sidelines.

I knew I would need to dress warmly if I was going to survive the elements. Over regular underwear, I put on thermal underwear. I wore a flannel shirt and heavy pants, a sweater, scarf, gloves, and a ski hat. I also wore my Army pea jacket and Army boots.

As I started driving toward the field, my only thought was: How was it possible that anyone could play a game in this weather?

The wind was blowing heavily and it was snowing and sleeting when I arrived at the field.

I had my notebook attached to a clipboard, but as the game started and as I began taking notes, the snow and sleet wiped out anything I had written.

When halftime arrived, I raced back to my car to warm up, but I could barely fit into the front seat since my entire body and my clothes were frozen like an icicle.

When the game resumed, I returned to the field, wondering even more when this misery would end.

Fortunately, the answer was shortly.

A St. Columbkille's runner was injured on the first play of the second half, and the game was called off.

When I returned to my apartment, I was greeted by my fiancée, Bunny. When I knocked on the door, she greeted me and said, "Oh, my goodness, get out of those clothes. There's no way you're coming into this house like that!"

It took me several minutes to rid myself of my frozen clothes before I entered the apartment.

In my career, I had several unusual experiences covering games, but never any as bizarre as the day I almost froze to death.

When I joined *The Salem News* in 1974, I covered Beverly High football. On Thanksgiving 1977, I covered the Salem-Beverly game that began with a tragic play.

Sophomore quarterback Mitch Carrier returned kickoffs for Beverly. As he was tackled on the opening kickoff at Bertram Field in Salem, he was injured. He was rushed to the hospital, where it was determined that he was paralyzed.

I covered Carrier's recuperation from the football injury, and while the injury was devastating, the reactions of people, not only in Beverly but all across the North Shore, were heartwarming.

Students from Beverly's vocational school built a ramp in Carrier's home, and people from many communities donated money to purchase a specially outfitted van that Carrier could drive.

Carrier went on to college and returned to Beverly High as a faculty member and a coach on the Beverly High football team.

I joined The Globe as a sports copy editor in June 1978 and became the school sports editor in January 1979.

Like many traditions, Thanksgiving football was not as popular as it once was, and over the decade of the 1970s, I noticed crowds seemed to be getting smaller each year.

We had about four pages of coverage for our Thanksgiving football games, and I felt that was sufficient to do a good job.

Alex Haley's book, *Roots*, became a television series in 1977, and America's passion for family and tradition was rekindled.

Crowds for Thanksgiving Day 1982 were very large, and I sensed a resurgence of interest in football on the holiday.

For our Thanksgiving coverage in 1983, I asked for eight pages for our Thanksgiving football pages, and we were given approval for the extra space. We covered more games and sent more photographers. Aside from the space, we needed additional copy editors and page designers.

For my final Thanksgiving in 1993, we covered twenty-three games and had photographers at ten of them.

The extra space meant a giant time and energy commitment from me. I rarely slept beyond 3 a.m. on Thanksgiving because I needed to be aware of weather conditions the morning of the games. If there was inclement weather, I was in the office at 6 a.m., calling athletic directors to determine if games were going to be played.

I needed to gauge if I needed all eight pages, or if I could use four fewer pages. I needed to make a decision by 7 a.m. because the size of the newspaper for the next day was determined at that time.

If weather wasn't an issue, I would cover a 10 a.m. game, return to the office, write my game story and begin to edit copy and lay out the eight pages.

The Globe was also responsible for compiling the ratings that determined which schools would qualify for the six high school Super Bowl games a week from the Saturday following Thanksgiving.

My reporters generally worked from 10 a.m. to well past 8 p.m. on the holiday.

The only restaurants that were open on Thanksgiving were those which served Thanksgiving dinner, so I arranged for our cafeteria to prepare a cart full of food—deli turkey, bread, potato chips, pickles, and brownies. They placed the cart in a walk-in refrigerator and gave me a key. At 3 p.m., I brought our "Thanksgiving dinner" to the sports department for our feast.

My workday ended shortly after midnight, when I returned home and had my dinner—a doggie bag prepared by friends Lena and Steve Saradnik, who had hosted my wife and son for the holiday.

When I arrived at the *Ventura County Star* as assistant sports editor in the mid-1990s, there was no high school football in California on Thanksgiving, and while I finally had the opportunity to take the holiday off, I declined.

After all, most of our family and friends were 3,000 miles away, and I had been working the holiday for so long it seemed strange to be off that day.

I started working on Thanksgiving, so a member of our staff could have the day off, but one year I decided that I wanted to make the holiday feel special for the people who had to work that day.

Anyone working on the holiday was invited to join us for a turkey dinner at the paper's cafeteria at 6 p.m.

My wife roasted a twenty-five-pound turkey and made a large batch of mashed potatoes. The Star provided tablecloths, utensils, paper plates, and sodas for our holiday meal, and anyone who came to the pot luck meal provided an appetizer, vegetable, or dessert.

In later years, invitations went out to anyone who was working and anyone who didn't have a place to go.

When Editor Joe Howry announced my retirement to the staff in 2006, his e-mail started out, "Sports Editor Larry Ames, who brought Thanksgiving to The Star, is retiring."

It was a fitting and fulfilling way for me to celebrate the holiday.

The Development Of 'Can't Miss' Prospects Ewing And Carpenter

Over the course of more than four decades watching the development of high school athletes, one area that interested me was how they matured as people.

I was always amazed at the maturity of Sarah Behn, the Foxborough High soccer and basketball standout, who, as a fourteen-year-old freshman, spoke more like a twenty-five year old woman. Behn scored 2,562 points in her high school basketball career and is the only four-time women's All-America basketball player at Boston College, which retired her jersey in 1988.

Behn runs a successful basketball camp that has seen more than 28,000 boys and girls advance their basketball skills and is the Brown University women's basketball coach.

Although they played different sports, I often compare the way basketball player Patrick Ewing and hockey player Bobby Carpenter developed their personalities.

Both were nationally known athletes in high school. We all knew Ewing was headed to the NBA and that Carpenter was going to be playing in the NHL.

Ewing was born in Jamaica and came to the United States in the seventh grade. At Cambridge Rindge & Latin, his coach, Mike Jarvis, didn't allow Ewing to speak with the media.

Jarvis and I began our careers at the same time in the mid-1960s. He was a student at Northeastern University, and his co-op job was as the sophomore basketball coach at Newton North High. I was the beat reporter for Newton North High at *The News-Tribune* in Waltham.

I told Jarvis that he was making a mistake by not allowing Ewing to develop as a person at the same time he was developing his massive skills on the basketball court.

"We all know where Ewing is headed, and by not allowing him to develop speaking skills and talking with the media, you are doing him a disservice. What happens if Ewing is drafted by the Knicks? He'll be eaten alive by the New York media."

During the post-season tournament in his senior year of 1981, Ewing was often heckled. The worst example came at a game against Boston College High, where fans taunted Ewing with the chant, "Ewing Can't Read."

Even more embarrassing was the news conference called for Ewing's announcement of his college choice.

As Ewing rose to speak, he had trouble getting the words out that he had chosen Georgetown University.

Ray Fitzgerald, The Globe columnist, focused his column the next morning on the subject of Ewing's awkward announcement. At Georgetown University, coach John Thompson continued the gag order. In fact, Georgetown's locker room was often a hostile place for members of the media.

My prediction did come true. Ewing was drafted by the Knicks, and he had a difficult relationship with the media for several years.

Ewing had the ability to communicate, but Jarvis and Thompson stifled an important part of his development.

Ewing was president of the NBA Players Association and was an excellent representative for his fellow players. He was an assistant coach in the NBA and was often a candidate for head coaching jobs. In April 2017, he was named Georgetown University basketball coach.

Carpenter, on the other hand, was comfortable with the media. As a senior at St. John's Prep in Danvers, Carpenter was on the front cover of Sports Illustrated. He was labeled "The Can't Miss Kid."

When Carpenter was drafted by the Washington Capitals as an eighteen year old in the first round of the NHL draft, he became the first American-born player to be taken in the first round, chosen at No. 3.

I attended his signing news conference in Landover, Md., in August 1981. Carpenter was at ease and eloquent in answering questions from the media.

I was the only member of the Boston media to attend the news conference, and many members of the Washington press corps asked me how an eighteen year old could be so poised.

"That's easy," I told them. "He's been talking with the media since the eighth grade."

Like Ewing, Carpenter had a long pro career, playing eighteen years. Since retirement, Carpenter has specialized in developing talent in the minor leagues.

His path to maturity was helped by his exposure to public speaking.

Educators and coaches need to develop promising athletes as people, as well as players.

Sinking The Jeep

Not all of my writing exploits were sports related.

During my tenure with the Massachusetts Army National Guard in the 26th (Yankee) Infantry Division, I served in the public information office at division headquarters at the Commonwealth Armory in Boston.

The PIO's function was to document, through news releases, stories, features, and photos, all activities of the division.

In the aftermath of Martin Luther King's assassination in Memphis in 1968, many of the National Guard units around Boston, were called into their armories.

In the event that troops were deployed into the community, our job would have been to document activity in the streets and to take photos.

We were told we would be setting up a command unit at White Stadium in the Roxbury section of Boston, where all Boston high school football games and track meets were held.

We were in our jeeps getting ready to head out to White Stadium when Lt. Gov. Frank Sargent, filling in for Gov. John Volpe, decided against sending the Guardsmen into the community.

Every summer, the 26th Division sent 15,000 troops to Camp Drum, N.Y., for two weeks of training, and our PIO office had a crew there to cover the training.

Because of concerns that there might be trouble in the minority community in Boston, 2,500 troops were sent to Camp Edwards on Cape Cod for the annual summer training.

In case there was rioting in Boston, the troops would be only ninety miles away from the city, rather than being 340 miles away in upstate New York at Camp Drum.

I was assigned to the troops at Camp Edwards, where my assignment that summer was to provide coverage in newspapers and on television and radio. Potential rioters would be led to believe a large segment of the division was training close to home.

Another year, my sole responsibility was to be with a Boston Herald magazine writer twenty-four hours a day during the summer training period at Camp Drum. The regular Army leadership at Camp Drum didn't want the writer roaming unattended.

One year I was assigned to Camp Drum to cover troops training in the field. Daily, my photographer and I headed out into the wilderness of Camp Drum (107,265 acres, 168 square miles) to cover the troops.

It had been a very rainy summer in Watertown, N.Y., and the dirt roads in the field were muddy. We came across an area with a lot of water, and I asked my photographer if he thought we could drive through it. He had his doubts, but I gunned the motor. The front of the jeep immediately sank into the mud. The rear of the jeep was pitched at a 45-degree angle out of the mud.

We were in the middle of nowhere, and all we could think of was taking a photo. My photographer jumped out of the jeep and took a photo of me standing up in the sunken jeep.

Fortunately, a farmer came along, and I gave him $10 to pull us out with his tractor.

Rather than risk any further consequences, we hastened back to headquarters, stopping first at the motor pool to hose the mud off the jeep before anyone could see us. We didn't want to face a court martial.

Delaney-Smith, Behn Show The Advancement Of Women As Players, Coaches

One of the greatest joys of my four-decade sports journalism career was the opportunity to see so many women and men grow into prominent positions in the sports world as athletes and coaches.

When I first started covering high school sports in the mid-1960s, there was little opportunity for girls to play sports. Many high schools offered only basketball and softball as girls' sports, and many newspapers didn't even allot coverage to girls' sports.

In the Boston area, most followers of prep sports referred to prep sports as "schoolboy sports."

So it is with great pride and enthusiasm that I watched and chronicled the careers of Kathy Delaney, now Kathy Delaney-Smith, and Sarah Behn.

I was at the Bishop MacKenzie Center in Newton on January 6, 1967, when Sacred Heart High of Newton's Kathy Delaney became the first girl in Massachusetts to score 1,000 points in a high school career. This accomplishment was made in an era of half court basketball with six players on each team and half the players not allowed beyond midcourt.

I was at Stonehill College on March 8, 1989, when Foxborough High's Sarah Behn fell two points short of setting the all-time state scoring record of 2,564 points. Behn hit a running jumper for a three-pointer with four seconds left to end her high school career with 2,562 points, one point shy of the overall record set by Cohasset's Bryan Edwards in 1988. She would have tied the record had she made the second of two free throws with twenty-three seconds to go in a 61-59 loss to Walpole in a sectional semi-final tournament game.

Behn was an All-America player in soccer and basketball at Foxborough.

Delaney played basketball for four years during the infancy of the women's basketball program at Bridgewater (Mass.) State College. She also competed for the Bridgewater State synchronized swimming team.

Behn, the Gatorade New England Player of the Year in 1989, went on to Boston College, where she was the first BC woman to surpass the 2,000 point plateau.

She set a Big East freshman scoring record (428 points) and was the league's Rookie of the Year. Sarah was the first Boston College player to earn All-America honors as a freshman. Behn is the only four-time All-America basketball player at Boston College.

As a senior at BC, Sarah became the women's basketball all-time leading scorer in the Big East, men or women (2,523 career points).

She was inducted into the Boston College Athletic Hall of Fame in 1998. In 2003, Boston College retired Sarah's jersey, the only female athlete at Boston College to be so honored.

It was interesting to observe the difference in the opportunities between the state's top high school basketball players in a twenty-two year span.

The passage by Congress of Title IX in 1972 was the impetus for opportunity for women in sports. Title IX prohibits discrimination against girls and women in federally-funded education, including in athletic programs.

While Delaney played in the pre-Title IX era, she was one of the pioneer high school coaches who was a moving force in making sure Title IX was followed in Massachusetts.

Ironically, when Delaney, who became Delaney-Smith when she married her husband, Francis, first applied for a teaching-coaching job upon graduation from Bridgewater State in 1971, she was seeking the swimming coaching position at Westwood (Mass.) High.

Westwood was seeking a jack-of-all-trades type of coach who could also coach girls' basketball.

Delaney-Smith was wary of taking the basketball position because she had played in the half-court era and had no idea how to coach full five-on-five basketball.

She needn't have worried.

Delaney-Smith compiled an incredible 204-31 record at Westwood, with six consecutive undefeated regular seasons and one state title.

Her major impact went beyond wins and losses. Delaney-Smith filed four lawsuits involving Title IX violations. Her actions affected areas such as salaries for coaches, playing conditions, and opportunities.

She became the Harvard women's basketball coach in 1982 and is entering her thirty-sixth season with the Crimson for the 2017-2018 season.

Following the 2016-17 season, Delaney-Smith has a 567-384 coaching record (330-148 in the Ivy League) with eleven league titles, six NCAA Tournament appearances, and six NIT Women's Tournament invitations.

Delaney-Smith's has coached for USA Basketball three times in her career, including serving as head coach of the team that won gold at the World University Games in Izmir, Turkey, in the summer of 2005.

Delaney-Smith was an assistant coach on the USA Basketball staff at the 2003 FIBA World Championships for Young Women, helping lead the U.S. to a gold medal in that tournament. In 2007, she teamed up with Temple's Dawn Staley and Holy Cross' Bill Gibbons Jr. to coach the USA team to gold at the Pan American Games in Brazil.

During the summer, Delaney-Smith runs a basketball camp, Crimson Elite Weekend, at Harvard.

Running basketball camps has been among Behn's major contributions.

After playing basketball professionally in Luxembourg, Behn founded the Behn Basketball Camps in 1994. Since then, more than 28,000 girls and boys ranging from six to seventeen have improved their basketball skills in full day, half day, and overnight programs at more than twenty locations in Eastern Massachusetts.

Behn coached basketball at her alma mater, Foxborough, and had Division II and III coaching jobs in college before becoming Brown University's basketball coach in 2014. Ironically, she is opposing Kathy Delaney-Smith's teams at Harvard.

Observing Delaney-Smith's and Behn's careers was one of the most interesting experiences of my career.

* * *

Before my arrival at The Globe, the heading above the two school sports pages every Tuesday, was Schoolboy Sports. The head was eventually changed to School Sports.

I made several moves to ensure girls would receive fair coverage in the paper.

Over sixteen years, I added eleven All-Scholastic teams and created The Globe Scholar-Athlete program for boys and girls. We expanded the Globe scholastic sports excellence programs by creating separate categories for Boston public school boys' and girls' programs and for boys' and girls' parochial school programs. I also created Male and Female Athlete of the Year Awards, which was announced at the All-Scholastic banquet. The award now honors my late Globe colleague, Will McDonough.

All championship finals in all girls' and boys' sports were covered, and regular season coverage and feature stories were based on merit, not on gender.

One winter season, sports editor Vince Doria called me into his office. "Am I imagining something, or are we giving girls' basketball more coverage than boys' basketball?" Doria asked.

"No," I responded. "We have been giving girls' basketball more coverage and features. Our girls' basketball programs and players are much better than the boys this year, and that's why they are getting more coverage."

I did receive some surprising criticism, though. When Globe sports copy editor Marcia Dick attended a conference for women's sports journalists, she returned from the conference with a surprising reaction to our coverage.

"Some women felt we were 'sucking up' to the women's constituency," she said.

Sometimes, you just can't win.

When I arrived at *The Ventura County Star* in 1996, there were All-County teams in football, boys' and girls' basketball, baseball, and softball.

Within three years, we had added an enhanced coverage by including all area teams in our All-County teams, created a Scholar-Athlete program for boys and girls, and established a Male and Female Athlete of the Year.

In my retirement column, on May 3, 2006, I was pleased that the advancement of girls' sports opportunities and coverage was a major change during my career.

Spending The Weekend
With Darren Flutie

Story ideas in newspapers come from a couple of sources. There are the original stories, and then there are the "borrowed stories."

One of my most interesting features came from a Cincinnati newspaper story via Globe Sports Editor Ernie Roberts. "One of the Cincinnati papers followed a high school football recruit during one of his college recruiting weekends," Roberts told me.

I liked the idea and began the process of finding a player to follow during the recruiting season of 1984.

If everything worked out, the plan was to run the feature on the front page of Sports Plus, The Globe's extensive Friday sports pages the weekend after the recruiting visit.

Before I actually planned the trip, I wanted to make sure everyone connected to the player was on board with the idea. I wanted the approval of the athlete, his parents, his school, football coach, and athletic director.

Finally, the most important approval had to come from the college itself and its head coach.

One of the most sought after players who was my No. 1 choice to follow was Pete Kendall, a guard from Archbishop Williams High School in Braintree, who had scheduled a visit to Notre Dame.

I couldn't have hoped for a better college to visit. Boston

College was the fan favorite in Boston, New England's only Division 1 college football team, but Notre Dame was a close second because of the number of Irish in the area and a large alumni base in Greater Boston.

The visit to South Bend appeared all but certain after everyone but Notre Dame had agreed with the plan.

The word from Notre Dame coach Gerry Faust was a dose of bad news. He wouldn't go along with it.

Faust's refusal surprised me because Faust had jumped from the high school ranks to Notre Dame, having coached the highly successful Moeller High football program in Cincinnati, Ohio.

Faust's selection had created much controversy. There were many who doubted a high school coach was capable of coaching in the college ranks.

With Kendall out of the picture, I went with my second choice, Natick's Darren Flutie, younger brother of Boston College quarterback Doug Flutie.

The approval process was quick and positive on all fronts, and I arranged to meet Darren at Logan Airport on a Saturday morning.

Flutie's recruiting trip was the second of his weekend excursions, but the hectic schedule was already taking its toll on him.

The previous weekend, the football, basketball, and baseball standout at Natick High had visited Duke. An overpriced croissant en route to his plane is all he had eaten until well after noon when he arrived at Duke's Durham, N.C., campus.

A tough 69-67 basketball loss to Bay State league-leading

Norwood the night before didn't enhance the early morning wakeup for the start of weekend No. 2 in his search for the right college.

Flutie dropped his luggage through the security check adjacent to Gate 12 at the Delta terminal at Logan Airport. He looked tired as he embarked on his official recruiting visit to the University of Maryland.

At least he wouldn't be hungry. Over a waffle and sausage breakfast on Delta Flight 203, Flutie looked ahead to his trip to Maryland with anxiety.

"It's funny, when I was a kid, I always said I wanted to play football for Maryland," he said.

Flutie was born in Manchester, Maryland, twenty miles northwest of Baltimore, and Bob Bates, a close friend of the Flutie family, had been urging Darren to play for the Terps.

The trip to Duke had been pleasant. A beautiful campus, the right responses from the coaching staff, and a scholarship offer at either running back or wideout had put Duke in the running for the Darren Flutie Sweepstakes.

Flutie also had a chance to talk with a pair of Duke football players—defensive lineman Harry Ward of Norwood and fullback John El-Masry of Waltham—both of whom Flutie had faced on the football field when he was a sophomore. Ward and El-Masry were happy at Duke, and they told Flutie they believe he would be happy there, too.

"Maryland said they projected me as a defensive back," said Flutie. "I'm confident I can be a running back or wideout."

Denny Murphy, a defensive coach and assistant coach in

charge of New England recruiting, was awaiting the arrival of Flutie and Lexington linebacker Jerry Montgomery at Baltimore/ Washington International. He had been in Boston on Wednesday to give the players their plane tickets and had a horrendous trip home, flying into Newark in a snowstorm and driving home from New Jersey on treacherous roads.

Murphy, who played and coached under Ara Parseghian at Notre Dame, directed the players into a 1984 Ford Tempo for the twenty-five-minute drive to Maryland's College Park campus.

In the next twenty-four hours, Flutie and Montgomery found out all the advantages of the University of Maryland.

Flutie and Montgomery were a few minutes late for a buffet at the Adult Education Center, a gothic-style building, typical of most on the vast, but well laid-out campus.

They were greeted by recruiting coordinator John Misciagna and head coach Bobby Ross. They were then escorted to the buffet. At 10:15 a.m., it was time for their second breakfast of the morning. Ross, a veteran college coach who spent four seasons as an assistant with the Kansas City Chiefs, came to Maryland two years earlier, succeeding Jerry Claiborne, who moved to Kentucky.

Ross said he would never forget his arrival as Maryland football coach. "I landed in Washington an hour before the Air Florida plane crash at the 14th Street Bridge," he said.

A native of Richmond, Va., Ross told the nineteen recruits of Maryland's proud academic record. "We want you to succeed academically as well as athletically," Ross said.

Maryland had two consecutive 8-4 seasons under Ross,

who pointed out that 1984 would be one of the toughest years ever, with the last three national champions—Miami, Penn State, and Clemson—on the Maryland schedule.

Ross painted a picture of Maryland football as a family. And throughout the weekend, the emphasis on closeness, friendship, and camaraderie was stressed.

Maryland called out two heavy hitters for the recruits' visit. U.S. Rep. Steny Hoyer, a liberal to moderate Democrat from Prince George's County in Maryland, and Washington Bullets' Tom McMillen were the speakers.

Hoyer cited the advantages of enrolling at Maryland. "You are only twenty minutes away from the heart of our government," said Hoyer, "and the Baltimore-Washington area is one of the business capitals of the world."

Hoyer, a Maryland alumnus, must have been the congressman in charge of area sports. Three years earlier, he welcomed Peabody's Bobby Carpenter to the D.C. area when the St. John's Prep star signed with the Washington Capitals at a Capital Centre press conference.

McMillen, the former three-time All-America basketball player at Maryland, was articulate, befitting his status as a Rhodes scholar. McMillen was also witty. "Just think, the President will be reading about you every day," he said.

McMillen said he considered attending North Carolina, one of Maryland's fiercest Atlantic Coast Conference rivals. "I told Lefty (Driesell) that the North Carolina library had more books than the Maryland library. He responded, 'So what? You're not going to read all the books anyway. And if you want more books, you can find all of them at the Library of Congress.'"

At each table were seated Spirits, the nickname the football staff had given Maryland coeds who escorted football recruits around campus. As the breakfast gathering broke up, Murphy told Flutie, "Your Spirit was a no- show. I'll be taking you to your appointments." It was Flutie's first disappointment.

The players were shepherded into an auditorium across from the buffet. They were shown Maryland's 1982 highlight film. It was a slick production, costing $35,000, and was of high quality. The film was like most such films, upbeat with quick-paced and high-energy music. It began with Ross strolling on the snowy turf at Byrd Stadium and ended with Maryland's 21-20 loss to Washington in the inaugural Hula Bowl on Christmas. Glimpses of some of the school's famous coaches were shown, including Bear Bryant, who directed the Terrapins to a 6-2-1 record in 1945.

Murphy, who was defensive coordinator under Neil Wheelwright at Holy Cross for a couple of years in the seventies, drove Flutie to his academic appointment in the science building. Murphy had trouble locating Room 417, but when he did, Dr. Martin Gannon, a young and enthusiastic professor, greeted Flutie with a smile and a handshake.

A week before, Flutie's academic session at Duke had been in pre-law, one of the majors he was considering. His appointment with Gannon was in his other possible major, computer science.

"You have to earn your way into computer science. The demand is far in excess of our current capability," Gannon told Flutie.

Gannon's presentation was full of computerese—chips, PC boards, bus, disks, memory, peripherals, tapes, and printers. Flutie, a B plus student in the top twenty percent of his class, looked lost.

As he and Murphy headed for the elevator, Darren mumbled, "It doesn't look like computer science."

After the academic appointment, Murphy drove Flutie to the players' living quarters. "We used to have all the players in a high-rise," said Murphy. "But by next year, all the players will be in newer dorms."

Flutie was directed into a dorm and was greeted by Frank Reich of Lebanon, Pennsylvania, a junior who was the heir apparent to graduating quarterback Boomer Esiason, Maryland's all-time passing leader. The cathedral-ceilinged apartment was neat and full of Maryland football memorabilia. On one wall was an autographed poster. It read: To Boomer and Frank, Good Luck. Clint Eastwood. "The players really like it here. You have your own bathroom, and you don't have to go down the long dorm halls," said Reich.

On the way to lunch, Murphy showed Flutie Byrd Stadium, where Maryland averaged a record 46,403 in 1983. "We're planning a new building where the press box is located," said Murphy. "We're pumping a lot of the money we've gotten from the bowl games the last two years into the program and the buildings."

Next stop was the Team House, official name for the college's football building. It was an old, but neat structure that had undergone some refurbishing.

As Flutie climbed the stairs to the second-floor lounge, he was stopped by an imposing figure. "Natick, huh," chortled Scott Fanz, observing Flutie's Northeast American Legion baseball championship jacket. "I'm from Hingham. Actually from Pittsburgh, but we moved to Hingham when my dad got a job in Boston."

It was Flutie's only hometown touch this weekend. There wasn't a Massachusetts player on the Maryland roster. "We just started going into New England two years ago," said Murphy. "The first Massachusetts player we went after was Dan Rice (the fullback from West Roxbury who chose Michigan)."

Fanz, a defensive lineman who played for Maryland for three years and was graduated in 1980, was the assistant strength coach. Fanz, who had a tryout with the Jets but was cut because of a recurring knee injury, ranked third in Maryland's 400-Pound Bench Press Club with 455, ten behind all-time leader Pete Koch, a defensive tackle who was the 1983 co-captain.

Fanz was graduated with a 3.8 (based on 4.0) average in the school of business, but his first love was conditioning, and when he had a chance to stay on with the Maryland program, he did.

Maryland pointed with pride to Danny White of the Dallas Cowboys as an example of their weight training program. White weighed 212 and bench pressed 260 pounds when he enrolled at Maryland. He left at 248 and bench pressed 450.

Lunch was typical of the weekend fare—quality and

quantity. The players were directed to the shrimp cocktail table and the buffet table full of cold cuts. There were plenty of soft drinks and rich desserts, too.

The 1983 highlights were shown. It was similar to the '82 film, but focused more on the exploits of Esiason and the Terps' 1983 Citrus Bowl appearance, a 30-23 loss to Tennessee. After the film was shown, Fanz provided a weight training demonstration. The players were then marched off to Cole Field House, to the second-floor football offices, where each player was interviewed by Ross.

As Flutie waited for Ross, he watched the Virginia-Clemson basketball game on a large-screen TV. As Clemson built a five- point lead with forty-two seconds left in the game, one of the Maryland football players yelled, "Boy, I hate to see Clemson win anything."

Clemson didn't win this day as Virginia's Othell Wilson stole an inbound pass with eight seconds to go and gave Virginia a 74-73 ACC victory.

Flutie never got to see the Virginia comeback because he was called into Ross' office.

The seventeen year old from Natick emerged twenty-five minutes later, armed with his second scholarship offer in two weeks. Flutie was pleased. His concern about being made a defensive back was unfounded. "Coach Ross told me they would play me wherever I wanted, if I could prove myself there," said Flutie.

The rest of Flutie's day was spent with fullback Richard Shure, a freshman from Pikesville, Maryland. After the interview with Ross, Flutie and Shure huddled together until dinner.

Dinner was at the Training Table, a recently redecorated dining hall. "Coach Ross has all the players here for mandatory breakfast and dinner," said Murphy. "Requiring them to come here for breakfast guarantees they'll be ready for the first classes of the day. It's more of an academic thing," he said.

Dinner started with another shrimp cocktail. The entree was prime rib and apple pie a la mode was for dessert.

The Maryland football staff was upset at the basketball team's home schedule. The football coaches liked to have the basketball team at home for the visit of the recruits because it provided an athletic touch to the weekend visit. But Driesell's team was on the road at Old Dominion this weekend, and the recruits just socialized for the evening.

Flutie didn't mind too much. He saw Maryland beat Duke, 81-75, a week ago in Durham, and Shure took Flutie to a Georgetown disco instead. Darren made it to bed by 2 a.m.

It was Super Sunday, and everyone around Metropolitan Washington was concerned about the Redskins, Joe Theismann, the Hogs, and the Smurfs.

Flutie and Montgomery rolled out of bed at 10:30 and greeted Murphy in the lobby of the Adult Education Center.

After the players selected their breakfast, Murphy asked who will win the Super Bowl. "It's going to be the Raiders," said Flutie. Montgomery nodded his head. "Yep, the Raiders."

Murphy gave the players two folders of Maryland football material. He had to drive a local recruit home and promised to return shortly. The players checked out of their room and met Murphy downstairs.

The players made their 12:15 p.m. plane, Piedmont Flight 358, with about four minutes to spare.

Flutie was tired and promised to head right to bed once he got home. As a flight attendant poured a Coke, Flutie looked back on the visit. "I was impressed with Maryland. I liked the fact that all the players got along very well, whether they were first team or fifth team."

His father was at the gate at Logan when the plane landed. Weekend No. 2 came to an end.

The following weekend, Flutie was in more familiar surroundings. He awakened Saturday morning with a cold, but he had played well the night before and Natick had beaten Milton, 49-41. There was no long trip for Flutie's third college visit. Boston College recruiting coach Barry Gallup, a bachelor who lived in Natick, was his chauffeur.

They arrived at BC's Roberts Center at 10:25 a.m. The handshakes with the coaching staff were accompanied by smiles. Darren was no stranger at Boston College, having visited often to see his brother Doug play quarterback for the Eagles.

Flutie and Gallup had breakfast together and returned to Roberts Center for an academic and weight training meeting. It was far more informal than Maryland, but that was BC's style of recruiting.

As Channel 38's film, "The Road to the Liberty Bowl," was shown, Doug wandered into the room. When the film was over, the out-of-town recruits were taken to Boston for a tour.

Darren and his host for the weekend, sophomore tight

end Carl Pellegata of Milford, Mich., headed for Pellegata's dorm room at Walsh Hall. Before they left, Gallup stopped Pellegata. "Make sure when you introduce Darren, don't say he's Doug's brother," warned Gallup. If BC was to land Darren, the issue of Doug being there must be downplayed.

When Pellegata and Flutie arrived at Room 201 at Walsh Hall, the place looked like any other dorm room would after a party. "It was a nice party," laughed Pellegata, an easy-going, low-key individual who was reportedly chosen by Doug to be Darren's host.

It was early afternoon, but sophomore running back Troy Stradford was still under the covers. "Get up, Troy," Pellegata told Stradford. "Darren and a reporter from The Globe are here."

"No comment," said Stradford, who didn't move.

Pellegata had suggested a game of basketball, but Darren turned down the offer because of his cold. Instead, Flutie, Pellegata, and roommate Ted Gaffney, a sophomore linebacker, shot the breeze in the dorm.

Flutie had dinner and caught BC's 91-78 rout of Seton Hall. It was then back to Room 201 at Walsh Hall for a party.

Fortunately, Darren's interview with head coach Jack Bicknell was scheduled for 1:30 p.m. The Saturday night party lasted until 5 a.m., and Darren didn't get up until 11 o'clock.

Flutie was happy about the interview with Bicknell. "He told me I would have been recruited even if Doug weren't my brother," said Darren.

Bicknell told Flutie he was definite Division 1A college material. Flutie now had three college offers to ponder.

Before Pellegata took Flutie to his dorm, he indicated his previous failure as host to recruits. "Nobody I've shown around has signed with BC," he said.

Late Wednesday night, his batting average went up. Darren Flutie decided to cancel his scheduled trip to Holy Cross that weekend and signed a letter of intent to enroll at Boston College.

"I liked Duke and I liked Maryland, but I chose BC because it felt like home. BC has a lot of talent on the football team, and I felt comfortable there. The other places were foreign; I didn't know anyone," said Darren.

Flutie then told all the colleges of his decision. There would be no more wooing and selling, and Darren was more at ease.

"Making the decision was like getting into the Super Bowl," he said.

For Darren Flutie, the toughest decision of his life was over.

Retiring With A Perfect Batting Average

The Globe's promotion department was always coming up with ideas to improve the newspaper's image in the community.

In September 1989, The Globe decided to bring Eddie Feigner and his traveling softball team to Boston to play The Globe's softball team that competed in a league comprised of other newspaper softball teams.

Feigner's team, dubbed "The King and his Court," was a traveling softball team of four players (a pitcher, catcher, shortstop, and first baseman). When Feigner returned from service in World War II, he couldn't find a job, so he created "The King and his Court."

It was a brilliant idea. Feigner and his team traveled around the world, similar to basketball's Harlem Globetrotters, and he and his team became worldwide celebrities.

I watched Feigner's team play on national TV a number of times, including on ABC's Wide World of Sports.

Feigner was the team's pitcher, and he could throw the softball more than 100 miles per hour. In more than 10,000 games, Feigner's team claimed 9,743 victories, 141,517 strike-outs, 930 no-hitters, and 238 perfect games.

In 1967, in a celebrity charity softball game, Feigner struck out Willie Mays, Willie McCovey, Brooks Robinson, Roberto Clemente, Maury Wills, and Harmon Killebrew—all in a row.

The game between "The King and his Court" and The Globe's softball team was played at the main softball field on historic Boston Common.

The Globe's team consisted of members of the sports department, some co-op students from Northeastern University who worked in the sports department, and Lisa Moore of Wellesley High, The Globe's All-Scholastic softball player of the year whom I had recruited to pitch for our team.

Although not a member of The Globe softball team, I was also in uniform that day. The only time I had ever competed on a team was as an eleven-year-old when I played in the Minor Leagues in the Dorchester Little League.

Feigner was sixty-four in 1989, and he pitched only a couple innings of the five-inning game. Despite his age, Feigner was still capable of throwing more than 100 miles per hour, and he dazzled the crowd of several hundred.

The rest of his court was three players from the Netherlands who appeared to be six-feet-four or taller.

When Feigner left the pitching mound, he was replaced by one of his teammates who appeared to be more than 6-7, and the speed of the pitches increased considerably. Needless to say, there was little contact made by The Globe's softball team.

In the fifth and final inning, I was told I would bat. My expectation was that I would take three pitches and sit down.

Pitch one blew by me in a whiz. Ditto for pitch two.

I stepped out of the batting box and came up with a strategy. I would start my swing before the pitcher released the ball. The idea seemed ridiculous, but I figured I had nothing to lose since I expected to strike out anyway.

As the pitcher began his windup, I began my swing. And to my amazement, and everyone else's, the ball hit my bat and dribbled a few feet down the third baseline. I rambled down the first baseline and reached the bag with a single.

My wife, Bunny, had been taping the game, so my first and only at bat as a softball player, had been preserved for posterity.

As the game ended, I announced my retirement, leaving my softball career with a perfect batting average.

The MIAA And Me

The creation of the Massachusetts Interscholastic Athletic Association, the regulatory agency for high school sports in the state, and my tenure as school sports editor at The Globe, came within six months of each other.

The MIAA was established on July 1, 1978, when the Massachusetts State Principals Association, the longtime regulatory body in the state, divided into the MIAA and the Massachusetts Secondary Schools Administrators Association.

I had joined The Globe as a sports copy editor in June that year, but in September, Sports Editor Vince Doria called me into his office and told me I would be taking charge of the high school coverage on January 1, 1979.

I was no stranger to the MSSPA. I had written a four-part series on the organization when I was at *The Salem News*, and I was familiar with Executive Director Bertram Holland, the retired Brookline High principal.

When I found out that I would become The Globe's school sports editor, I called Holland and asked if I could meet with him and Dick Neal, the former Pope John High athletic director and basketball coach who was the new executive director of the MIAA and the MSSAA.

Our meeting at the MIAA's office in downtown Boston was cordial. I explained that I would be taking over as the paper's school sports editor, the first time in the paper's history that an editor, not a writer, would be in charge of the paper's high school coverage.

"I plan to cover the MIAA's meetings just as a political reporter would be covering the state legislature," I told Neal and Holland, who was staying on until the first of the year to train his successor.

"I feel it's important to report on your activities. Your regulatory decisions affect the lives of all student-athletes, and I want to keep the public informed," I said. "I understand as a regulator your decisions aren't always popular, but I when call I would hope to get answers. I don't want to have to make several different calls to multiple sources to get answers to my questions."

Furthermore, I told Neal and Holland I planned to cover the MIAA's monthly board of control meetings. All proposals made by the executive staff had to be approved by the board, made up mostly by principals, but also including superintendents of schools, school committee members, athletic directors and coaches. The Massachusetts Interscholastic Athletic Council served as the body where MIAA policies and rulings could be challenged.

It didn't take long for the rancor between the MIAA and me to develop. In January 1979, I wrote a feature that pointed out MIAA regulations provided obstacles for opportunity to deaf student-athletes.

There were several times that year that requests for information were denied by the MIAA.

I told the MIAA that, as an agency that determined the fate of high school athletes and high school sports teams, its records were public.

The MIAA did not have direct legislative authority to regulate high school sports, and MIAA counsel Roger Dowd told me their position was that the organization's records were not public.

The MIAA received its authority in the same way as the NCAA, whose member colleges pass along their regulatory powers. Massachusetts state law states that school committees have the power to regulate high school sports but may pass that authority to an authorized representative, which is the MIAA.

I challenged the MIAA's opinion on public records in 1980, and six months later, John McGlynn, supervisor of pubic records in the Secretary of State's office, ruled in my favor. My complaint was based on the MIAA's refusal to provide a document I had requested.

I covered every MIAA board meeting and reported on the organization's decisions and regulations.

In May 1980, at the meeting where the MIAAs annual budget was announced, I perused the budget and noticed salary increases for the executive staff. Since I had covered every board meeting, I couldn't understand how I could have missed the pay increases.

After the meeting I asked a member of the board when the raises had been voted, and he replied that during the annual meeting on April 3, the board had met privately and voted the raises.

I surmised that the MIAA didn't want me to know about the raises and had met privately to avoid my scrutiny.

So, on behalf of The Globe, I filed a complaint with the state Attorney General's office claiming the MIAA should be subject to the state's open meeting law.

Despite a positive ruling on my behalf, The MIAA stone-walled the Attorney General's office, but finally capitulated, agreeing to post notices as a standing policy.

Although the case was settled with a positive outcome, the attorney general's office was not pleased with the MIAA's behavior. In a Massachusetts Newspaper Publisher's Association bulletin in January 1981, the MIAA's delay in agreeing to comply with the open meeting law was criticized.

"Assistant Attorney General Ernest P. DeSimone has closed the case but he may share the opinion of many others that the MIAA soft-peddled what had been a flagrant violation of the law. Three of DeSimone's letters went unanswered over a period of several months and it was not until the Massachusetts Association of School Committees read the riot act that the MIAA finally responded, albeit weakly."

The most troubling decision the MIAA board ever made came in October 1980, when it found Don Bosco was innocent of a rules violation.

In July that year, I received a call from a parent who was concerned that his son refused to be with his family during their annual two-week vacation on Cape Cod.

"The Don Bosco coach is conducting summer practices at South Boston," the parent told me. "I'm a working stiff, and this is my only vacation of the year. I know these practices are illegal, but I can't do anything about it."

MIAA rules don't allow coaches to conduct practice once the season ends. Coaches are only allowed one offseason meeting with his players, but are not allowed to hold practice until the official starting date.

Since the field is barely a mile from The Globe office, I stopped by the field that afternoon to watch the illegal practice.

When the practice ended, I walked up to assistant coach Steve Fratalia, extended my hand and said, "Hi, I'm Larry Ames of The Boston Globe, and what are you doing here?"

The coach had no answer, so I returned to the office, and I wrote a column on the illegal practice. What I observed was clearly a practice, and that was what I wrote.

The MIAA could not gloss over the infraction, so it asked Don Bosco to investigate the matter and report to the board at the next meeting.

Don Bosco didn't deny the illegal practice. but came up with a defense that head coach Ron Lewis was a fine person. The school also presented the board with a list of athletic officials who wrote glowingly of Lewis.

Lewis said that he had attended almost all of the weekly summer practices, commonly known as "Captain's Practice," and that he had conducted three meetings with his team even though MIAA rules stipulate a coach can only conduct a single one-hour meeting with a team out of season.

To my complete shock, the MIAA board found Don Bosco not guilty of the violation on a 5-3 vote.

So much for integrity.

Another time, the MIAA board voted to go into executive

session, which I challenged. "The purpose of your going into executive session is not covered by the law," I told the board. "Don't let me stop you from going into executive session, but any vote you take will be overturned when I file a complaint with the attorney general's office."

The board remained in open session. I had many squabbles with the executive staff and board over the years.

In 1988, the MIAA declined to give umpires a $3 a game raise despite the fact the umpires had been without a raise for a long time. High school baseball games often went beyond three hours and were often played in chilly weather, and I backed the umpires bid for a raise, arguing that the schools pay umpires' fees, and the MIAA only pays the umpires during the playoffs.

I further argued that Neal had received a $6,000 raise that year, and the umpires certainly deserved a $3 increase.

Accompanying my column was a cartoon by Larry Johnson that depicted Neal sitting on his desk smoking a cigar that read $6,000 raise while an umpire stood in front of him holding a tin cup that read: $3 raise. Johnson's caption was a classic as he had Neal smoking his cigar and proclaiming, "We can't afford a raise."

In February 1988, the wrestling officials threatened to go on strike if they didn't receive a raise.

I spoke with the officials and MIAA Associate Executive Director Sherm Kinney, who was in charge of wrestling, to get an idea of what was going on. After several calls to both sides, it was apparent that neither side was speaking to each other, ad that I was the only one speaking to either side.

The major complaint of the wrestling officials was that the MIAA wouldn't even negotiate with them, and if that continued, they wouldn't officiate any meets, meaning the cancellation of the wrestling season.

I was uncomfortable with the back and forth discussions with me since journalistic standards call for newspapermen to report on the news, not make the news.

However, since both sides were talking with me and not with each other. I didn't want to have the wrestling season ended because of stubbornness, so I asked the officials if they would return to work if I could get the MIAA to sit down with them. They agreed.

I called Kinney and told him of the compromise I had worked out. He conferred with Neal, who refused the compromise.

I told Kinney it wouldn't look good if I reported that the wrestling season had to be canceled because the MIAA wouldn't even sit down with the officials, so Kinney and Neal finally agreed to the compromise.

The MIAA and the officials met, thus saving the season. A settlement was reached on the salary boost that avoided any future problems.

Over the years, the MIAA has made several controversial decisions and rulings.

I never could understand how they operated. Its goal was to better school sports in Massachusetts. Often, I found that wasn't always the case.

Reviving The Bus

In the 1970s, The Globe beefed up its scholastic sports coverage.

In addition to its games coverage, notebooks, and All-Scholastic teams, the paper created two weekly School Sports pages, utilizing four correspondents, generally gleaned from the Northeastern University co-op students in the sports department.

The pages also featured more coverage of girls' sports and the banner on top of the first page was changed from Schoolboy Sports to School Sports, although many old timers still refer to high school sports in Eastern Mass. as schoolboy sports.

When I took over as school sports editor in 1979, I was always looking for a way to bring more attention to the pages.

Ironically, one of the most popular ideas I had was reviving an old feature of The Globe's coverage.

From 1938 until his death in 1952, Gene Mack, The Globe's sports cartoonist, ran a weekly feature called The Bus.

The purpose of The Bus was to chronicle the remaining undefeated football teams from week to week. The undefeated teams were ceremoniously removed from the bus.

Mack's bus was actually a convertible, but it was a highly popular feature, eagerly awaited by Globe readers every week.

In 1982, I decided that bringing back The Bus would be a great idea.

I sat down with Globe sports cartoonist Larry Johnson who agreed to take on the job of drawing The Bus.

We agreed that we didn't want to copy Gene Mack's convertible bus, and we needed to modernize it, so Larry drew a real bus that would list on the side of the bus the undefeated football teams in Eastern Mass.

Larry came up with a scruffy looking bus driver who smoked a cigar, but we eventually dropped the cigar because some readers protested that it was not proper to have a school bus driver smoking a cigar.

We also felt we needed someone to throw the week's losing teams off The Bus.

Larry came up with the perfect dog, but we still needed a name for him. Out of the blue, I came up with the idea of Exit, and so The Bus idea was complete.

Johnson drew The Bus from 1982 until he left for *The National* in 1989, when Globe artist Jim Venable took over the task.

In the fall of 1994, when Venable's first Bus of the season appeared on the School Sports pages, all the losing teams were dropped from The Bus, but for the first time, Exit ceremoniously dropped an individual from The Bus—me. I had left The Globe in June 1994.

Serving On The Red Auerbach Youth Foundation

Even before the Red Auerbach Youth Foundation was established, I was already an unofficial contributor.

Globe colleague Will McDonough created the foundation, which honored the legendary Celtics coach and president. McDonough planned a massive $500,000 fund-raising gala for the foundation, but he wanted to sponsor a couple of events so the public could see what type of programs the foundation would be supporting.

He asked me to come up with the ideas for a couple of programs. One was a clinic before a Celtics game, and the other was a freshman-sophomore track meet, which has run annually since its inception in 1983.

So it was no surprise that I was named to the board of advisors of the foundation.

I served on a number of scholar-athlete scholarship committees and was a founding member of the board of directors for the Bay State Games, but I was honored to be part of a group that would be working on behalf of youth in Greater Boston, but with a large focus on the city of Boston.

Members of the board ranged from Celtics officials to lawyers, civic leaders, and prominent businessmen.

Our board meetings focused on how we would spend the foundation's money, which was aided every year by a Celebrity Golf Tournament, among other fund-raising activities.

At one board meeting, one member suggested we provide a two-week overnight summer camp experience for boys and girls throughout Boston.

The consensus on the camp idea was very positive, but one member cautioned that we should check with youth leaders across the city to see if it would work.

At our next meeting, youth leaders from the black and Asian communities attended our board meeting.

A representative from the Boys and Girls Clubs of Boston told us that while the idea was a good one, it would not be practical.

"There are a lot of single mothers in the black community who depend on their older children to watch their younger siblings. These mothers often work two or three jobs, and they would never agree to send their children to overnight camp for two weeks."

The Asian community representative said the camp idea would not work. "Many of these families were boat people escaping from their native countries. They would never trust anyone with their children for two weeks."

The youth representatives suggested that the best way the foundation could support youths in Boston during the summer would be to fund a number of day trips, and that's what we did.

In the ten years I served on the board, Auerbach attended only one meeting. It was held on a Sunday morning in the Celtics office on Causeway Street, across from the Boston Garden.

Although I had attended many Celtics games as a youth and had covered the Celtics on occasion for *The Salem News* (after Red had retired), I had never met Auerbach before.

I was in awe of Auerbach, one of the strongest personalities in the history of sports. You either loved Auerbach (if you were a Celtics fan) or hated him (if you were a fan of all the other teams). With nine NBA titles in eleven years, Auerbach was the most successful NBA coach of his era. He annoyed opposing teams and their fans when he lit up a victory cigar once a Celtics win was assured.

One of the most popular Red stories was that during the winter, Auerbach would shut off the heat in the opposing team's locker room while turning up the heat in the Garden during the spring playoffs. The Garden was built in 1928 and had no air conditioning.

Red was the master and one-man ruler. No one would dare question him.

At one of the Auerbach Celebrity Golf Tournaments, Celtic great Tom "Satch" Sanders told me one of his favorite Red stories. "Red would call you into his office and say, 'On Sunday you are going to go and speak at this youth group's breakfast.' Athletes could make a lot of money giving speeches, but we were expected to do this without any compensation. Nobody could say 'no' to Red."

As the meeting started, Red was in a nasty mood. The annual golf tournament had just been held, and there were a number of things that irked him. Needless to say, all of Auerbach's concerns were dealt with the following year.

I thoroughly enjoyed my time with the Auerbach Foundation, and when I left The Globe in 1994 and headed west, Celtics vice president and general manager and Auerbach Foundation chairman Dave Gavitt sent me a thank you note and a personalized Celtics jersey.

"This is just a short note to say a thousand thank you's for all the great things you have done to help our efforts to provide Auerbach Foundation programs that are meaningful to the young people in our state. Quite frankly, I don't know where we would be without you, and we are going to miss you.

"In the larger sense, your substantial contributions to our efforts are but a small part of a splendid career of service and excellence devoted to our young people. You have made a difference, and that is something that cannot be said but for a few special people."

Dealing With Death On A Daily Basis

Newsprint readership has declined as the Internet has reduced interest in reading a printed copy of newspapers.

One area of the paper that has maintained readership is the obituary pages. People want to know who in their communities have passed away, and they want to be able to express their condolences. Plus, the obituary is the last time a person's life is chronicled.

So while newspapers' main roles is to report news like politics, business, society, food, and sports, dealing with deaths is considered an important area, and one area where propriety and sensitivity are vital.

The Vietnam War was going strong when I became a newspaperman. Very often, newspapers were the first to inform families that their loved ones had died in the war.

My first experience with writing about a death came in 1968 when standout Newton South High athlete Danny Mendelson died on June 21 as a result of complications from gall bladder surgery. I had known Danny since his first football game as a sophomore in September 1966.

When I climbed the stairs to the press box at Fitchburg High, I was greeted by Danny's father. "Look out for Danny Mendelson tonight," he said.

Danny was the starting fullback that night because the starter had been injured. Danny gained seventy-nine yards in a 7-0 loss. It was the beginning of two stellar seasons for Mendelson.

Mendelson was also a standout baseball player and had just been named to The News-Tribune All-Suburban League baseball team.

News-Tribune Sports Editor Frank Murphy was the only columnist in the sports section. His regular column was titled "The Sports Realm." But Murphy was on vacation when Mendelson died, and it was up to me to write his eulogy.

Danny was a beloved student on campus. He was popular with the student body and with the faculty, an unusual combination in a time of student rancor and distrust during the Vietnam War.

English teacher Jonathan Slater wrote of Danny, "He would burst into my classroom, all granny glasses, bell bottoms, and grins. I would smile, always. You had to smile. There stood a kid so full of life, so pleased, so pleasing that you had to respond—and you did. You enjoyed his special summertime that we so seldom dare embrace in our lonely, cautious little worlds."

I was nervous because this was my first column, and it needed to reflect the unique young man who died way too early. The column was well received. A year later there was a memorial concert for Mendelson and an announcement that a Danny Mendelson Memorial Fund had been created.

At the same time, a memorial plaque was hung on the wall outside the Newton South High gymnasium. On the plaque was my eulogy.

During my time at The Globe, the paper ran appreciations on the lives of local, legendary sports figures who had died.

Because the school sports constituency was more than 300 schools, I was often called on to write the appreciations. The eulogies consisted of the deceased's accomplishments; thoughts from coaches, athletes, and friends; and my knowledge of the deceased.

I worked particularly hard on the appreciations. My words in the largest newspaper in New England would be the final pubic recognition of a person who was beloved beyond family.

I was particularly proud to have been chosen to write the appreciation when former *Salem News* Sports Editor Tony Romano died in 1993. I had worked with Romano at the Salem paper, and he was well-known and respected, particularly in New England professional golf circles.

I was out of the office most of the day when Tony died, but when I returned, fellow assistant sports editor Robin Romano, informed me of her dad's death.

"I would be proud if you would write dad's appreciation," Robin told me.

"I would be honored to do so," I replied.

I knew most of the people I eulogized extremely well, and while I was saddened by their deaths, I was pleased to have had the opportunity to recognize their life's achievements.

When Conflict Of Interest Surfaces

A lot of the rules about loyalty to employers and conflict of interest issues have changed in the last two decades.

For the longest time, newspaper sports reporters and editors were not allowed to take outside employment or make appearances on a radio or television broadcast without permission.

It was considered a conflict of interest if a writer took an assignment with a media competitor or with an organization. Even an assignment that raised a potential conflict of interest could be rejected by employers, who felt that they controlled what you could and couldn't do.

I was caught in that situation twice in my career.

Because of my knowledge of high school sports, Massachusetts Gov. Edward King wanted to appoint me to the Governor's Council of Physical Fitness and Sports in 1979.

The Globe refused permission because there would be a conflict if I found it necessary to write a column on the council.

When the Bay State Games asked me to join their Board of Directors in 1983, The Globe gave me permission.

The Games, which conducts Summer and Winter Games, has been very successful. From modest beginnings, the Summer Games features more than 7,000 athletes in twenty-six sports. The Winter Games were established in 1985.

I had enjoyed my time on the Bay State Games board, until March 1986.

Oil Can Boyd, a pitcher for the Boston Red Sox, was in UMass Medical Center in Worcester. All of the baseball writers were in spring training, so I was sent to Worcester to speak with Boyd.

At the hospital, I inquired if I could speak with Boyd. Instead of getting an answer, I was confronted by a security guard.

"You have to leave the hospital," the guard told me.

"I represent The Globe and I am in a public building. You have no right to tell me to leave," I said.

"Dr. Pappas ordered me to have you removed from the hospital," the guard said.

Dr. Arthur Pappas, the head of UMass Medical Center, happened to be the Red Sox team physician and he also happened to be chairman of the Bay State Games board of directors.

With that, I left the hospital.

The next morning, I called Bay State Games Executive Director Doug Arnot and resigned from the board.

"I happily joined the board and have felt I contributed to the success of the Games," I told Arnot, "but yesterday a conflict of interest surfaced, and I can't remain on the board."

Ironically, much has changed in the last couple of decades. Many sports reporters appear on radio and television broadcasts, often as regulars.

Even many newspapers also own cable channels and have their reporters appear regularly.

Gruff And A Graduate Of The Lou Grant School Of Journalism

When I joined *The Boston Globe* in June 1978, I fully expected that my writing career was over.

I had been hired as a sports copy editor, and while I was pleased that after twelve years, I had finally been hired at my dream newspaper, I was anticipating long night hours working on the copy desk.

I spent my first six months at the paper working the "lobster shift," toiling from 1 a.m. to 9 a.m. to help put together the sports section for The Globe's evening edition.

In September, I was called into Sports Editor Vince Doria's office for a meeting. Doria told me that School Sports Editor Neil Singelais, a Globe veteran since the 1940s, was becoming a general assignment reporter and that I would become the school sports editor on January 1.

High school sports had been my main focus at *The News-Tribune* in Waltham and at *The Salem News*. Also, I had spent six years working sports at *The Boston Herald* one or two days a week.

Doria explained that all previous school sports editors had been writers, and that my focus would be as a supervisor of four of the Northeastern University co-op students who worked in the sports department and wrote for the school pages.

"We wanted an editor who could hire, train, and supervise the writers and develop their writing skills to be able to produce copy that was strong enough to appear in a metropolitan paper," said Doria.

Aside from hiring the school sports writers, I would edit their copy, assign stories, and edit and make up the two Tuesday school pages and the weekend Sunday school coverage.

Doria, one of the leading sports editors of his era, made it clear that I was in charge of the school sports section, and that I didn't need to check with him about anything.

"We knew when we hired you that this was where you were going to land. You were born in the city, went to school here, and know the school landscape as well as anyone," said Doria.

When I left Doria's office, I was pleased with my new assignment, but I had no idea what was ahead for the next fifteen and a half years.

What made my new assignment intriguing was that there was no blueprint for the assignment. I was free to create the procedures, policies, guidelines, and organization.

During my tenure as the school sports editor, and within five years as the assistant sports editors/schools, I adopted policies that ranged from behavior on the job, ethics, phone call procedures, deadlines, dress code, punctuality, writing style, and do's and don'ts.

Early on, I wrote some controversial features and started writing a school sports column. I added eleven All-Scholastic teams in my tenure, including the Scholar-Athlete team.

I assisted the promotion department in putting together the annual All-Scholastic banquet that honored our All-Scholastic athletes and coaches. I started finding our national speakers and added former All-Scholastics who had continued their success in the college and professional ranks as part of the banquet speaking program.

Within a short period of time, I also hired, trained, and supervised all the co-op students in the sports department, took on payroll responsibilities, occasionally was in charge at night, and filled in during the morning and afternoon department head meetings.

I worked closely with my four writers, and I realized in a short period of time that I was becoming a mentor, and that meant a lot to me because my development as a journalist was a result of many who had taken me under their wing.

I created leadership opportunities for the school writers and prepared them for their future careers. I made them accountable and responsible.

I took my role as the supervisor of The Globe's co-op students very seriously. While my policies and demeanor upset a number of people in the sports department, I believed my responsibility was to make the four school writers and all the co-op students in the department ready for their future on their first day of their first job.

If a co-op student was a minute late, I'd sit them down and ask them why they were late. "It was only a minute," they'd respond. "Late is late," I said.

When one co-op was forty-five minutes late during a snowstorm, I sat him down, too. "Haven't you looked outside? it's snowing," he said. I told him, "When the weather is bad, you leave early. It's no sin to arrive at work early."

In 2011, Nell Scovell, a successful television supervising producer, wrote in the web site *Grantland* of her experience in the sports department at The Globe. She called me "gruff" and "a graduate of the Lou Grant School of Journalism."

Since I came along first, it should have been Lou Grant was a graduate of the Larry Ames School of Journalism.

Writers needed to defend what they wrote. Often, when I was editing a story, I would question a writer about authenticity. Occasionally, I would get an "I assumed" or "I figured" or "I guessed" response. So my favorite retort became, "Never assume, figure, guess, or think you know something. Either you know or you don't know."

I never tolerated excuses. Writers would sometimes use the expression, "I tried," when they failed to complete a story. Nothing made me more furious. "There is no trying in journalism."

Working for me meant being on call twenty-four hours a day. I once called Kevin Hughes and asked him to work on a project that I needed the next day. He came in at 8 p.m. and finished the project at 5 a.m.

"I hate you," he wrote in a scathing e-mail when he left the office.

I e-mailed him back, "Thanks for the great job. I picked you because I knew you were the right one to do it."

When the springtime changing of the clock was scheduled for the following Sunday morning, I called the school writers to remind them to set their clocks ahead so they wouldn't be late to take standings calls on Sunday afternoons.

Jill Reilly took offense at my call. "Of all the things you've done, this is the worst. Don't you think we know enough to change our clocks?"

A few years later, I received a call from Reilly, who was working as spokesman for the Boston Police Department. "I had to call you, Larry, because yesterday I was late for work because I forgot to change my clock."

My writers worked long, hard hours. During tournament time, the hockey writer would often cover four tournament games a night.

When Ian Browne started his career at CBSSports.com in New York, his boss asked for a volunteer to cover a basketball doubleheader at Madison Square Garden. Only Browne volunteered for the job. "My boss asked me why I volunteered when no one else wanted the assignment, I told him, 'That's easy. I covered a whole day of hockey tournament games for Larry Ames, and this is a snap.'"

Browne is MLB.com's Boston Red Sox beat writer and author of one of the most successful blogs in the country. He is the author of "Idiots Revisited," looking back at the 2004 season when the Red Sox ended the "Curse of the Bambino" with their first World Series title in 86 years.

My most grueling assignment came during the fall tournament season. I called for a volunteer to cover the two Friday night state field hockey finals at WPI and the six state championship soccer games, also at WPI, the next day.

The "lucky" writer who took on the assignment and made deadline for the eight games would be the school writer's captain the following year. The captain would be in charge of schools when I was away from the office.

As difficult as the assignment was, there was always a volunteer for the job, and in every year, each writer did a great job, making deadline and producing great stories.

B.J. Schecter was one of the captains who became one of the top editors in the country. Schecter joined *Sports Illustrated* as a reporter-researcher right out of Northeastern University and was executive editor of SI.com and editor of Campus Rush. He was also a professor of journalism at several colleges, including Columbia University.

Todd Archer volunteered to cover one of the few Thanksgiving Day games that weren't postponed because of a blizzard. Today, he's ESPN.com's beat writer for the Dallas Cowboys.

One of the school writers who didn't venture far is Scott Thurston, who became a sports copy editor upon graduation from Northeastern and is now senior assistant sports editor at The Globe.

Many other current and former school writers have served on The Globe sports copy desk. The long list of successful graduates includes four lawyers.

Success was not restricted to the co-op students who wrote for the school section. Many of the co-ops who answered the phones and did a variety of important functions within the department have also had successful careers.

Deanna McGovern Penn was hired by Tufts Health Plan the day she was interviewed for her first job. "They asked me how I could be so polished and so ready for work right out of college," said Penn, now a vice president of Liberty Mutual Insurance Company. "I was trained by Larry Ames."

I was never a candidate for Mr. Popularity. In a decade and a half of supervising college students, I was invited to one graduation party.

Time has changed the opinion of many who were my greatest critics.

Aside from being a father and grandfather as a septuagenarian, my greatest joy is seeing the success of the "Ames graduates." I have kept in touch with a lot of them and have kept tabs on most of the others.

Partial List of Ames graduates

B.J. Schecter

Professional in residence for sports media and business programs Seton Hall University

Executive Editor Baseball America magazine

Former Executive Editor SI.com

Former Editor, Campus Rush

Scott Thurston

Senior Assistant Sports Editor The Boston Globe

Ian Browne

MLB.com reporter Boston Red Sox

Author, "The Idiots Revisited"

Todd Archer

Dallas Cowboys beat writer ESPN.com

Jim McBride

New England Patriots beat writer The Boston Globe
Former Sports Copy Editor The Boston Globe

Bob Fedas

Sports Copy Editor The Boston Globe

Ed Ryan

Head of Display Advertising The Boston Globe

John Conceison

Sports Copy Editor Worcester Telegram-Gazette

Rhiannon Potkey

University of Tennessee football beat writer Knoxville News-Sentinel
Former Ventura County Star sportswriter

Deanna McGovern Penn

Vice President Liberty Mutual Insurance Co.

Dan Nowak

Sportswriter New Haven Register

Paul Doyle

Sportswriter The Hartford Courant

Tom D'Angelo

Sportswriter Palm Beach Post

Michael Mayo

Dining Out Critic Sun-Sentinel Fort Lauderdale
Former News, Sports Columnist Sun-Sentinel Fort Lauderdale

Chris Burt

Lead Designer Cox Media Group, West Palm Beach, Fla.

Mark Jaworski

Sports Editor Fort Wayne Journal Gazette

Bill Doherty

Former Assistant Sports Information Director Northeastern University

Substance Abuse Counselor St. Elizabeth Hospital, Boston

Mark Singelais

Sportswriter Albany Times-Union

Jill Reilly Gillis

Public Relations Director Goodwin Procter LLC

Nell Scovell

Television Supervising Producer

Steve Richards

ESPN copy editor

Jeff Horrigan

Senior Writer Hoffman York

Founder Director Hot Stove Cool Music

Former Boston Red Sox beat writer The Boston Herald

Ben Sturtevant

Marketing and Communications Manager Midcoast Regional Redevelopment Authority

Matt Bannen

Administrator Bridgewater State University

Arthur Anastos

Vice President and Managing Counsel Dunkin' Brands

Tatiana Fish

Press and Industry Analyst Hewlett-Packard

Tina Cassidy

Journalist, best-selling author

Vin Sylvia

Director of Marketing and Communications The Sylvia Group
Former Sports Editor Manchester Union Leader

Jerry Higgins

Internal Communications Specialist North Carolina Division of Motor Vehicles
Former Carolina Hurricanes Public Relations Director

Sean Hennessey

Associate Director Boston College News and Public Affairs Department

Mike Barba

Customer Care Supervisor, Comcast Cable

Ken Gordon

Massachusetts State representative (D) Bedford
Lawyer

Mike Biglin

Sports Copy Editor The Boston Herald

Ed Giulotti

Asst. Wire Desk Team Leader Gannett Nashville Design Studio

Ken Carty

Asst. Vice President Communications Natixis Global Asset Management

John Bisognano

Senior Editor Digital Palm Beach Post

Cory Nightingale

Sports copy editor Miami Herald

Rick D'Errico

Director of Communications and Client Services Buzz Media Solutions

Jocelyn Taub

Sports/Travel writer
Traditional & Digital Marketing/Promotion/PR/Branding/ Events in broadcasting/sports/music

Michael Hurley

NESN blogger

The True Value Of Mentoring

When I retired as a sports journalist on May 3, 2006, I fondly recalled my rookie years as a sports reporter.

After working as a part-time reporter for *The News-Tribune*, a small 16,000 circulation newspaper in Waltham, Mass., for nearly two years, I was hired full time on December 7, 1966.

Sports Editor Frank Murphy welcomed me with this piece of advice: "Remember, you can't get married during football season."

Thus began the learning process that continued for forty-one years, first as the mentored and finally as the mentor.

When Murphy died on October 23, 2015 at age ninety-three, I was quoted in two appreciations of his life.

Recalling his contributions to journalism and the communities he served for nearly five decades as sports editor, provided me with a newly appreciated perspective of my training and how he molded me into the journalist I became.

Murphy was strictly old school. He always followed rules and guidelines. He believed in principles and propriety. I learned the right way to be a journalist as he directed my path.

The News-Tribune had a reputation as a training newspaper. When a mistake was made, it was treated as a learning experience.

I was called into Managing Editor Tom Murphy's office after I had misspelled liaison in a story. He asked me to spell the word, and I gave him the same misspelling that appeared in my story.

"The shame is not in not knowing the word, but that you didn't look it up. That's why we have a dictionary," said Murphy, Frank's older brother.

It is a lesson I carried throughout my career, and I must have told that story to young writers a hundred times.

Frank Murphy was beloved by his readers and the athletes he covered because he was always supportive and never negative. When asked why he never criticized, he responded, "That's not my job."

His work ethic was unmatched, and all of his traits were passed on to me through his example.

In my 1987 Boston Globe column praising him on his retirement, I wrote, "Working with Murphy was an education. You didn't call in sick, even when you were. A snowstorm or blizzard was no excuse for missing work; you found a way to get there. If Murphy could walk to work in a hurricane and toil in the dark by the Coleman lantern, then you got in—somehow."

In 1974, I left *The News-Tribune* and joined *The Salem News* sports staff. Four years later, I was hired by The Globe on June 6, 1978 for what I thought was going to be a career as a sports copy editor on the night desk.

What I didn't know was that The Globe had plans for me.

In September 1978 I was called into Sports Editor Vince Doria's office and was told I would become the school sports editor on January 1, 1979.

The Globe's school sports editor had always been a writer. However, the Globe decided it was time to hire an editor who could hire and train a writing staff for the school sports pages on Tuesdays and for game coverage and features.

Although I thought my writing career was ending, it was actually being revived.

I started writing a high school column. Instead of covering a few communities, the breadth of The Globe's vast circulation increased the scope of coverage to more than 300 schools.

I valued the platform I had been handed, but when I saw a wrongdoing or an issue that needed to be addressed, I didn't hesitate to be critical. I thought of Frank Murphy's philosophy of never being critical, but I realized that by adhering to the principles of fairness and proper journalistic standards I could make a positive contribution with my column.

Through the years my role at The Globe expanded. I hired and trained all of the paper's co-operative students from Northeastern University and other colleges, and I had other administrative duties. In 1983, I was promoted to assistant sports editor/schools.

Teaching was a huge part of my job training the high school staff. I was now passing along the journalistic principles Frank Murphy had provided me.

I felt a great responsibility to provide the college co-ops with the best training and education I could provide. I had guidelines, rules, procedures. I was strict and not very popular.

But I went beyond the call of duty and helped many of our co-ops find their first full-time jobs. And I've kept in touch with most of them or followed their career paths. Many landed on the Globe sports copy desk. Four became lawyers.

In July 2016, I had lunch with one of my former co-ops, Todd Archer, who is ESPN.com's Dallas Cowboys reporter.

"You know, Larry, you told me years ago that many of the co-ops had become copy editors at The Globe, but none had ever become writers at the Globe. Well, Jim McBride has switched from the desk to become one of the Patriots' beat writers," said Archer.

I was overjoyed to learn of McBride's new assignment, and I sent him a congratulatory e-mail.

His response pleased me even more. He thanked me for my role in helping him become a journalist. "You were hard, but you were fair. You taught us to be accountable and responsible, and that's what I'm doing with my own kids."

My son, David, has become a mentor, too.

He played lacrosse at the Rivers School in Weston, Mass., and at the University of Arizona. Since graduating from college, he has been a high school lacrosse head coach and assistant coach for seventeen years. At Dublin Jerome High in Dublin, Ohio, his teams won three state titles and reached four other state championship games. Twice he was named U.S, lacrosse assistant coach of the year.

His specialty is defense, but his other specialty is mentoring. One year, seven of his players became Division I college lacrosse players. Often, he reconnects with many of his former players whom he has steered in the right direction.

B.J. Schecter, one of my former co-ops and former executive editor of SI.com, was a mentor at SI. He also mentored students as a professor of journalism at several colleges.

As someone who greatly benefited from being properly trained and has had the joy of mentoring, I strongly believe every college student should be assigned a mentor, not just a guidance counselor. Particularly today, when it so much harder to find niches in the workplace, being trained and steered in the right path has become more valuable.

The Young Journalist
Is Coached To Success

I was fortunate to receive excellent newspaper training, but a big part of who I became was my daily contact with coaches and athletic directors.

A year after I started with *The News-Tribune* in Waltham, I was assigned to cover Newton North High.

The Newton school system was often considered to be among the top public schools in America. Part of the reason for the high ranking was its administrators and teachers.

Newton North's athletic director was Reggie Smith, a wise and crafty administrator who knew who to hire for his coaching staff.

Smith was a strict follow-the-rules guy who had the uncanny ability to get his way in every manner, yet the other person actually believed it was his/her idea.

When Newton North built a new school in 1970, Smitty got his way when he convinced school authorities to build an open space rather than a gym. The only separate facility was a basketball court with seats.

It was a novel idea at the time, but one that was embraced by many down the road.

I spent a considerable amount of time with Smith, and I learned a lot from him. He might have been lecturing, but it didn't feel that way.

In my daily dealings with Newton North coaches Jim Ronayne (football and golf) and Norm Walker (football and wrestling) Howie Ferguson (baseball), Al Fortune (boys' basketball), George Jessup (gymnastics, boys' tennis and training) and Lem Boyle (track), I learned about the proper way to do everything.

They were all strong educators aside from their duties as coaches. Their student-athletes benefited from their skills as teachers and coaches.

They not only had successful programs but they also knew how to get their athletes into the right schools for their talent and their academic level.

Just being around them was an education for me.

I spent a lot of time with Ronayne and Ferguson.

Ronayne was a former Marine who was also a colonel in the Marine Corps Reserves. I always referred to him as "The Colonel."

He was strict and rigid, but if you went along with him, he would go to the end of the world for you. He had contacts in colleges all over America, and coaches trusted his judgment.

Ferguson was a legendary baseball coach, who prepared and planned with meticulous efficiency.

In twenty-three seasons as Newton's head coach, Ferguson posted a 334-117-7 record with twelve Suburban League titles, four Eastern Mass. titles, and one state championship.

He scouted future rivals in a time when no one else did; he analyzed his players with every possible statistic.

As *The News-Tribune* reporter covering Newton baseball, I sat alongside Fergie on the bench and kept the scorebook, as all my predecessors did.

At night, Fergie would call me to get each player's statistics. If I ruled a player had a hit, he would ask me why that certain at-bat wasn't an error. As a result, I had to be as accountable to Fergie as his players were. When he didn't agree with me, I had to defend my decision.

Fergie would call at 11 p.m. and 7 a.m.

Today, coaches rarely have to wait long before becoming head coaches. Fergie came to Newton North in 1933 as a social science teacher and assistant baseball coach and became head coach when Jeff Jones left to become a scout for the Boston Braves in 1948.

Imagine having two head baseball coaches from 1927 to 1970.

From 1969 to 1975, I was a part-time sports information director, for three years at Bentley College and for three years at Brandeis University.

At Bentley, I worked with Al Shields, who was the school's athletic director and men's basketball coach. At Brandeis, my supervisor was Athletic Director Nick Rodis.

Both were capable and successful men who would teach me more than I could ever imagine.

Bentley had moved into its Waltham campus just four years before I became its SID. The college had been in Boston before and had no campus.

Bentley played its basketball games in Waltham before getting its own facility in the 1970s.

Shields had done an incredible job developing Bentley's basketball program. Bentley was often ranked highly in the

New England Division II rankings, but it had never cracked the United Press International's national Top 25 ratings.

Shields pushed me hard to get national recognition. I sent out weekly releases nationally, and when we were scheduled to play Long Island University in Brooklyn, I visited all the New York dailies pushing for coverage.

In my second year at Bentley, I received a call from UPI in New York that Bentley was ranked No. 11 in the country that week. It was the college's first time in the national Top 25. It was a personal triumph, but Shields deserved the credit because he drove me to the success.

Rodis was an international expert in sports. His Harvard roommate was Kenny O'Donnell, future special assistant and appointments secretary to President John F. Kennedy.

When Kennedy took office, Rodis joined the State Department, where he served until Kennedy's assassination in 1963. Rodis was also actively involved in the World University Games.

Rodis was a humble man who accomplished much behind the scenes. When the United States wanted to resume diplomatic relations with China, it was a ping pong tournament between the two countries that broke the ice.

President Richard Nixon called on Rodis to negotiate the tournament details with the Chinese.

I once asked Rodis how you negotiate with the Chinese.

"You sit down with them, they tell you what you will do, and then you do it," he said.

Rodis always provided excellent direction and advice. He gave me the best advice I ever received.

In my final year at Brandeis, my wife, Bunny, became pregnant.

"When the baby is born, go to the bank the next morning and open a savings account. Put money away every week, and when you can, keep raising the figure," said Rodis.

We followed his advice, bought dividend paying stocks and faithfully put money away. When our son was ready for college, we had saved enough to pay for his tuition.

Helping Gatorade Honor
The Nation's Best Athletes

I had the honor of serving on more than a half dozen scholar-athlete committees, and I also served on the board of directors of several other organizations.

But when my phone rang in 1984, I was asked if I was interested in helping to select athletes of the year in a number of states.

The caller was Bruce Weber, publisher of *Scholastic Coach Magazine* in New York.

Weber explained that he had been hired by Gatorade to establish a program that honored the best male and female athletes in all fifty states and the District of Columbia. In addition, a national Athlete of the Year in each sport would be selected.

The awards were going to be given for boys' baseball, boys' football, girls' softball, girls' volleyball, boys' basketball, girls' basketball, boys' cross country, girls' cross country, boys' soccer, girls' soccer, boys' track, and girls' track.

Selection would be based on three criteria: athletic achievement, academic excellence, and exemplary character.

My assignment was to be the selection advisor for the six New England states.

I liked the idea of a national organization honoring high school athletes, but I was concerned that Gatorade would sponsor the program for a year or two and then drop it.

I asked Weber if Gatorade intended this program to last beyond a year or two. "Gatorade intends this to be a program for a long time," he told me.

I joined the program at its inception in 1985, assembling a number of high school sports editors to assist in the selection in the five other New England states besides Massachusetts.

I was on the board of advisors from 1985 until 1994 when I left The Globe.

My involvement in the Gatorade program wasn't over, though. I received a call from Weber at my Ventura County Star office in the spring of 1996.

Weber was looking for a restaurant in the county to host a dinner for Gatorade National Girls' Track Athlete Kim Mortensen of Thousand Oaks High in Ventura County.

I made a recommendation to Weber, who invited me to the dinner. We had a chance to renew acquaintances and talk about the program.

A few months later, Weber called me. "Our West Coast advisor is leaving the program, and we would like you to rejoin the board," he said.

I told Weber that I had a lot more contacts in New England than I did in California, which was a major task by itself because of the size of the state.

"You're a founding member of our group, and you'll be able to figure it out," said Weber.

I agreed to rejoin the board, gathering contacts throughout California and across Oregon, Washington, Arizona, Alaska, and Hawaii.

The West Region was a bigger challenge than New England. Aside from the size of California, there were challenges in Alaska, whose football season ended before the end of October, and in many of the Western states, where soccer was played in the winter, rather than in the fall, where it is played in most of the country.

I served on the board until my retirement in 2006, serving long enough to see a new twist to the program in 2003.

In the first major change, a National Male and Female Athlete of the Year was established.

The prestigious annual award is presented at a luncheon in Los Angeles in the afternoon before the annual Espy Awards.

In 2003, the National winners were basketball standouts LeBron James of Akron, Ohio, and Candace Parker of Naperville, Ill.

My wife and I were fortunate to meet the initial National Athletes of the Year and to enjoy watching their careers take off: James as the NBA superstar and Parker as a WNBA standout.

The Gatorade program has thrived in more than thirty years since its inception, and I was proud to play a small part in helping establish an award to honor high school athletes.

My future wife, Bunny, and I celebrate our engagement in November 1971. We've been married for 45 years.

This is my official Boston Globe Speakers Bureau photo.

In October 2015, at a gala celebrating the 20th anniversary of the Reggie Lewis Track and Athletic Center in Roxbury, Mass., I was presented the Persistence Award for my 11-year effort that helped make the building a reality. From left, Roxbury Community College President Valerie Roberson, me, Massachusetts Gov. Charlie Baker, Reggie Lewis Track and Athletic Center Executive Director Keith McDermott.

This photo accompanied my story on Katie Lynch in The Boston Globe in March 1992. Katie, who was born with a form of dwarfism, demonstrated that athletes were differently abled, not disabled.

Joan Lynch, Katie's mother, displays The Boston Garden Good Sport Scholarship plaque awarded Katie between periods of a Boston Bruins game. I was chairman of the selection committee.

Covering the troops of the 26th (Yankee) Infantry Division during summer training at Camp Drum, New York, was one of my duties as part of the Public Information Office of the division. During a rainy summer, I believed I could navigate my jeep through a "puddle." Fortunately, a farmer with a tractor came along and rescued my photographer and me.

I was the part-time sports information director at Bentley College for three years. Al Shields, the Bentley men's basketball coach and athletic director, was an influence in my growth as a journalist.

As a member of the B'nai B'rith New England Sports Lodge, I helped found the annual All-Scholastic Breakfast that honored outstanding Jewish high school athletes in Eastern Massachusetts. Here, I address the honorees.

My interview skills were tested by athletes such as Joe Namath and a greyhound competing in the annual Wonderland Park Derby.

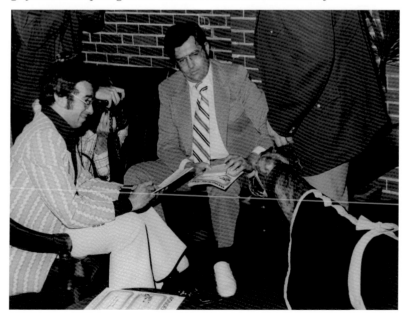

The Boston Globe softball team took on Eddie Feigner's famed "King and His Court" in a 1989 game on historic Boston Common. Although not a member of the team, I, third from right in the second row, dressed for the game. I singled in my only at bat.

My 17-year-old son, David, and I had a great time during our 11-day baseball trip in 1992. Right, I took this photo of David before a game between the Baltimore Orioles and the Chicago White Sox at Camden Yards in Baltimore. Left, in 2014, I took a photo of my grandsons Vance (left) and Kaden at an Orioles game against the New York Yankees. Ironically, both photos were taken in nearly the exact same spot in the stadium.

This Larry Johnson cartoon accompanied my Boston Globe column that criticized the Massachusetts Interscholastic Athletic Association's failure to give state umpires a $3 raise per game. The umpires did receive their raise.

Cartoon courtesy of The Boston Globe

The Bus, a weekly cartoon that listed all undefeated football teams and those teams that were dropped from The Bus, was revived in 1982. Larry Johnson drew this cartoon to accompany a story that announced the return of the feature. The original Bus had been drawn by famed cartoonist Gene Mack from 1938 until his death in 1952.

Cartoon courtesy of The Boston Globe

Following the 1983 high school football season in Eastern Massachusetts, Boston Globe sports cartoonist Larry Johnson presented me with the season-ending Bus as a souvenir.

Cartoon courtesy of The Boston Globe

SECTION THREE
COMMENTARY

Could The Cost Of Pro Sports Bring On Its Doom?

In preparing this book for publication, I went through a number of photographs taken by my photographers while I was on assignment.

I came across a photo of me with New York Jets quarterback Joe Namath and Newton North High quarterback Dick Dezotell. The photo was taken at the 1967 New England Sportsmen's and Camping Show at Hynes Auditorium in Boston.

Namath was being paid $427,000 a year by the Jets, but Namath probably didn't get paid more than a couple of thousand dollars for his appearance that day. I earned $3,744 that year.

If Namath were making that appearance today, his fee would most likely be in the tens of thousands of dollars, if not more. His salary alone from the Jets would be more than $20 million a year.

When the New York Titans (eventually Jets) were awarded an American Football League franchise in 1959, the franchise fee was $25,000. Today, the Dallas Cowboys are worth $4 billion.

When George Steinbrenner bought the New York Yankees in 1973, he paid $8.8 million for the franchise. Its worth today is $3.4 billion.

When I was an eight-year-old attending pro games in Boston, I paid 75 cents (bleachers) to $1.50 (unreserved grandstand) a game to see the Red Sox play at Fenway Park. I paid 85 cents to sit in the second balcony to watch a Boston Bruins game at Boston Garden, and the cost of the cheapest seat at the Garden to see the Celtics was $1.50 (behind the basket seats in the balcony).

When the Boston Patriots began play in 1960, an end zone ticket was $2.50 and a box seat was $5.

Many great athletes of the 1950s and 1960s barely earned more than $20,000 a year, and even greats such as Ted Williams and Joe DiMaggio earned roughly $100,000 a year. In the 1960s, even the highest average salaries declined.

The best way to explain the huge difference in ticket costs, is to take a look at Red Sox prices from the mid-1990s until the present. In 1994, the year I left The Globe, I received The Globe's four box seats to a Red Sox game. The seats were to the left of the visiting dugout, seven rows from the field. The Globe paid $14 a seat per game for the season tickets.

We requested and received tickets for the same four seats to a Memorial Day game against the Cleveland Indians in 2007. The cost of the tickets had escalated to $125 apiece.

Red Sox owner John Henry bought *The Boston Globe* in 2013. The following year, Henry, as Globe owner, didn't renew The Globe's tickets. Instead, Henry, as Red Sox owner, sold the four season tickets, at $175 each, meaning he received $56,700 a year for selling the tickets instead of spending $56,700 a year for buying the tickets. That's how you become a billionaire.

Going to a Patriots game is no longer $2.50. Single game tickets range from $77 to $350 a seat face value. But the reality is that most tickets are bought on the secondary market and can cost from $175 to $1,250 a seat.

Parking at Gillette Stadium in Foxborough is costly and will run you $40 a car per game.

Concession prices have gone beyond skyrocketing. Hot dogs cost between $6.50 and $8, and beer prices range from $7 to $12 apiece in many stadiums.

So how did we arrive at this insanity?

The best example of the outrageous costs is a quick look at the Los Angeles Dodgers. The current Dodgers owners bought the team for $2 billion.

The 2016 payroll at the start of the season was $227 million.

Pitcher Clayton Kershaw, considered the best pitcher in baseball, signed a seven-year, $215 million contract with the Dodgers, and in 2016 he earned $32 million.

He earned more than $1 million a start and was paid more than $10,000 a pitch.

Millions of Americans, earning $10 an hour for their 40-hour work week, are paid $20,800 a year before taxes, just two pitches for Kershaw.

Presidential candidate Bernie Sanders gained popularity in 2016, calling for a political revolution and advocating a minimum wage of $15 an hour. This would result in an annual wage of $31,200, just more than three pitches for Kershaw.

As Kevin O'Leary of *Shark Tank* says when an entrepreneur cites a ridiculous valuation for his business, "Stop the madness!!!!" We, as fans, may someday say the same thing when it comes to supporting pro sports.

Athletes 'Sneaking Up' As Multi-Millionaires

During a break at a coach's dismissal hearing in 1982, I had a chance to speak with John O'Neil, the Converse Rubber Company's president. O'Neil was testifying at a school committee meeting which I was covering.

I had known O'Neil for a few years because of Converse's sponsorship of the annual Eastern Mass. Shriners Football Classic.

During our conversation, I learned a lot about O'Neil. He said he had worked his way through Tufts University, toiling on the overnight shift at Converse.

We discussed how much the cost of sneakers and athletic footwear had increased dramatically over the past few years.

"Our company made its reputation with the Chuck Taylor basketball sneakers," O'Neil said. "A number of years ago, the sneakers were selling for $9.95 a pair. Our marketing people told us we would have to increase the price of the sneaker to $10.95 or $11.95 a pair in order to remain profitable.

"We held meeting after meeting, debating whether we could raise the price and whether the public would be willing to spend double figures for a pair of sneakers."

It seems almost ludicrous to think that a one- or two-dollar increase would create such corporate consternation, particularly with the huge cost of sneakers today.

In 2014 and in subsequent years, NBA Hall of Famer Michael Jordan has made more than $100 million a year as his portion of Nike Air Jordan sales. There are 226 styles of Air Jordans, ranging roughly from $100 a pair to $499.99 a pair.

In 2016, Jordan, who owns 90 percent of the Charlotte Hornets, was worth $1.4 billion, according to Forbes. Jordan earned only $94 million in his fifteen-year NBA career.

Jordan isn't alone in cashing in on sneaker endorsements. While the nation debated a $15 minimum wage in 2016, athletes have become multi-millionaires with outrageous salaries and endorsements of sneakers.

How To Avoid The Fergusons And Baltimores

Once the Reggie Lewis Track and Athletic Center opened in 1995, I visited the building a few times over the years.

Although my wife, Bunny, and I had moved to the West Coast in 1994, I attended the official opening. I marveled at the wonderful track surface and the wall plaques that housed the names of all the inductees of the Massachusetts State Track Coaches Hall of Fame, of which I was an honoree in 1988.

In 2003, my family and friends gathered at a ceremony when the press room was named in my honor.

In other visits, I made it my business during the track season to stop by and watch a meet.

But in 2015, in the twentieth year of the Reggie Lewis Center, I visited the building three times, learning so much more of what the building had become.

In March, I returned to the Reggie Lewis Center with Steve Forman, a friend from California who had been born and raised in Dorchester, as I had. We had come to Boston to visit our old neighborhood.

We ran into Keith McDermott, the Lewis Center's executive director, who gave Steve a tour of the building, citing the features and programs, some of which I was unaware.

During that visit, McDermott told me that there was going to be a 20th Anniversary Gala in October, and that I would be honored for the role I played in getting the facility built.

In June, my wife and I stopped by the Reggie Lewis Center to be interviewed for a video that would be shown at the gala.

While we were there, McDermott escorted us into a senior exercise class where a large group was taking a break. McDermott said there were one hundred seniors registered for the class, which met for two hours, three times a week. Before the class started, the seniors walked around the track.

But the real awakening for me came at the gala, where I was honored with the Persistence Award. There were 700 people in attendance at the gala, which included a reception, dinner, awards ceremony, and concert by the Manhattans.

I was pleased to see a large contingent of coaches and friends, many of whom I had not seen for more than two decades. Massachusetts Gov. Charlie Baker, who was the honorary chairman of the gala, and Boston Mayor Marty Walsh were also on hand to support the gala, but the group that impressed me the most was the large throng of citizens from the minority communities of Roxbury, Dorchester, and Mattapan who were there to celebrate THEIR building.

The original intent of the building was to house a track facility that would serve the athletes in Boston and the state for practices and meets.

It became that and much more. College students also used the facility, and the U.S. Indoor Track Championships have been run on the track several times.

The building has also served as the indoor athletic facility for neighboring Roxbury Community College, whose athletes had never had an indoor home.

But one of the Lewis Center's major values is the use of the building for political, social, and civic purposes as well as concerts and many other events.

Roxbury Community College President Valerie Roberson cited the value of the Lewis Center. "More than 1.2 million people pass through these doors every year," she said.

Speaking to many people at the gala, I was impressed with how much ownership each person had in the building.

Massachusetts State Track Coaches Association executive director Frank Mooney, who, along with the late Bob McIntyre, was honored with an endowment in their names, pointed out that the community was so proud of the building that in twenty years not a single window had been broken and not one bit of graffiti had been placed on its walls.

Before I was presented with my award, I was advised that I should speak for two minutes.

"I am a product of Roxbury and Dorchester, and I believe it's important for people to remember where they came from," I told the audience. "Unfortunately, many people who grew up in the inner city, and who have thrived, have forgotten their roots. I did not want to be placed in that category, and that's why I pushed for so long to make this wonderful building a reality." I also said there was a great need in our country to build facilities such as the Reggie Lewis Center to improve the quality of life in the inner cities.

"If we had more Reggie Lewis Centers across America, we wouldn't have had the unfortunate situations we experienced in Ferguson, Mo., and Baltimore," I concluded.

Like many urban areas in America, Boston has issues, but because of the Reggie Lewis Center, issues rarely boil over because they have a place to discuss and settle matters before they explode.

Riots cause death and destruction, and it costs a fortune to clean up and deal with upheaval.

It's time for our political leaders to spend money on more Reggie Lewis-like centers to make urban areas of America better places to live.

My Advice To Graduates

I gave this 1992 commencement address at Newman Preparatory School in Boston:

Thank you.

Commencement is akin to an athletic event in that it is a climax to a long journey, yet there is another game tomorrow.

When you receive your diploma tonight, it will signify the successful conclusion of a long period of study, many trials and tribulations, several ups and downs, and many victories and setbacks.

No matter whether you were the valedictorian or just an average student, the achievements of yesterday are but memories tomorrow. For while it is understandable to gloat or reflect on accomplishments, to succeed in the long run means greeting each tomorrow with as much or more enthusiasm than you greeted the previous day.

As a writer and editor for twenty-seven years, each day I must prepare for tomorrow's edition, but once the presses start rolling, all of the hard work, dedication, and enthusiasm is over. Immediately, the next day harkens with the same challenges staring at you.

We live in a fast-paced society. When I started my career, we were still editing type the same way type was being set at the turn of the century. With our technology today, we have super computers, and we utilize satellite technology.

Just the other day, Bud Collins filed his tennis column from the French Open. In a matter of seconds, his story came over phone lines from Paris. Twenty years ago, his story would have taken hours via Western Union.

Your parents have told you about the right path to take. Study hard, finish high school, and go to a good college. If you do the right things, good things will happen to you.

Not too long ago, I heard Northeastern basketball coach Karl Fogel tell a group of high school students that doing the right thing may not guarantee success.

Because of our economy and because of competition, he said that being just as good as the next guy may not be good enough. Competition dictates that we achieve to our highest levels.

The Bruins found out just that last week when, after soundly beating Montreal in the Adams Division finals, they were no match for the vastly superior Pittsburgh Penguins, and they were swept out of the NHL playoffs.

The Celtics were similarly dispatched by the Cleveland Cavaliers. In each case, the tomorrows will be future seasons, and there will be calls for a higher level of achievement.

I am often asked what I consider to be the most important attribute of high school sports, and while there are many, the one I always choose is the ability to learn how to lose.

Competing in sports teaches us how to win, camaraderie, patience, dedication, etc., but learning how to lose is most important because in business and life, learning how to bounce back from defeat is essential.

You may have heard the expression that tomorrow is the first day of the rest of your life. No matter what transpired yesterday or today, there is always the promise of tomorrow's sunshine.

There is a misconception that one person can't make a difference, but I don't believe that. Because of the large school constituency at *The Globe* (more than 300 schools), I annually meet thousands of people. Many are people who have made a difference by having confidence and by having a cause or belief.

Take Joe Lazaro, for example. The national blind golf champion from Waltham started a golf championship nearly twenty years ago, and his tournament has raised hundreds of thousands of dollars for Lions eye research. Joe was blinded by a land mine in World War II, and he could have lived his life feeling sorry for himself. Instead, he married, raised a family, and became an important part of the Waltham and Greater Boston community.

Recently, I had the opportunity to write a story abut a courageous young lady, Wayland High junior Katie Lynch, who was the school's track and wrestling manager. That in itself is not unusual, but Katie is only twenty-eight inches tall. Because of a genetic disorder, she has undergone more than a dozen life threatening surgeries, yet she has a bright outlook on life. She does not view herself as a disabled person, but as a person who has different abilities. Her courage has been an inspiration to others.

Just think how much better a society we would be if everyone could just show one person a kindness each day. It is not only a terrific thing to do but also fulfilling.

We can also be fulfilled by remembering those who made it possible for you to reach this point. Think about the many friends and relatives, coaches, tutors, etc., who took time to help you reach this important night. Once you have found your niche in life, be a contributor by giving back as much as you have received, if not more.

And, finally, remember to honor your parents for they have sacrificed much to get you to tonight's commencement.

Congratulations on your achievement. Tonight, bask in your moment and celebrate.

Tomorrow, be ready for your next challenge.

Thank you.

Before the commencement speech, my wife, Bunny, and I celebrated our twentieth wedding anniversary by having dinner with the Newman Prep administrators.

Been There, Done That

May 3, 2006
By LARRY AMES
Ventura County Star

A lot has changed since I first entered a newsroom in January 1965.

Newspapers were printed much the same way they were in the late nineteenth century. Stories were written on type-writers, and copy was edited by pencil.

Type was set in hot lead by large, ancient linotype machines, editors used glue to piece pages together, and grumpy city editors wore green visors.

More than forty years ago, little changed in newspaper copy. Washington was first in peace and last in the American League, the NBA was eight teams, and women were mostly excluded from the sports pages.

As I conclude forty-one years as a sports journalist, the greatest achievement in the newspaper business has been fair treatment of girls and women and more coverage of sports other than football, basketball, and baseball.

In 1965, girls prep basketball players played half court basketball and had little or no recognition in most newspapers across the country. Fortunately, that changed in 1972 with Title IX, and with it, the newspaper industry went along.

The most evident change can be seen in women's basketball. The NCAA women's tournament and Final Four is televised.

Girls who had no basketball life after high school now have college and professional (WNBA) ball to which they can look forward. Equal access to the sports pages has also been provided for sports such as track and field, tennis, golf, soccer, volleyball, and water polo.

Over the years, The Star has developed programs such as All-County, the Scholar-Athlete, and The Star Cup. In all cases, girls and women are given the same treatment as boys and men.

Forty years ago, standings, statistics, and polls were rare. Today, they are commonplace.

As a sports reporter, I was privileged to cover Game 6 of the 1975 World Series between the Boston Red Sox and the Cincinnati Reds. It was also the longest day of my career. I started working at 5:45 that October morning and went to bed at noon the next day. Carlton Fisk's home run in the 12th inning beat the Reds at 12:34 a.m. Working for an afternoon paper, the Salem News, provided me with more time to write. A colleague and I left Fenway at 3 a.m., and I didn't finish my assignments until nearly 11 a.m. Five hours later, I headed back to Fenway Park for Game 7.

I also covered Game 5 of the 1976 NBA Finals between the Boston Celtics and Phoenix Suns, a triple overtime classic won by Boston, 128-126.

I have also been privileged to work in Ventura County the last ten years. The local, national, and world accomplishments of athletes coming from an area of only 800,000 people are inspiring.

As a sports fan, I saw the last seven years of Ted Williams' career and attended the first game played in the American Football League in September 1960. The Denver Broncos defeated the Boston Patriots that night. I paid $2.50 to sit in the end zone at Boston's Nickerson Field (formerly Braves Field).

I saw nearly all the Bill Russell-Wilt Chamberlain battles in Boston, was there the night Havlicek stole the ball, and was in the Boston Garden the day Bobby Orr gave the Boston Bruins the Stanley Cup.

I have enjoyed working with some of the most dedicated people I have ever met—the men and women coaches and athletic directors at high schools and colleges who help nurture our future leaders.

I consider all my colleagues over the years—reporters, editors, photographers, composing room personnel, imaging specialists, and our advertising sales people and circulation workers—to be a big part of my extended family.

My greatest privilege has been assisting in putting out a quality daily product for the reader. I have met hundreds of thousands of people in more than four decades, and I thank all of you for enriching my life.

SECTION FOUR
THIS AND THAT

Insight From Banquet Speakers
Eruzione, Jones, Ashe

For the longest period of time, The Globe hosted a banquet honoring the paper's All-Scholastic athletes and coaches of the year. The athletes, their parents, and coaches were invited to the event at the Copley Marriott in Boston. More than 1,500 attended each year.

After the meal, a fifty-minute audio-visual presentation featuring the athletes was shown, followed by a talk by a famous national or international athlete or coach. Over the years, we added a former male and female All-Scholastic athlete who had gone on to collegiate or professional excellence.

One of my tasks was lining up the featured speaker. Some years the job was easy, but in other years there were a number of obstacles to overcome.

In 1981, the obvious choice was Mike Eruzione, the Winthrop native whose goal in the 1980 Winter Olympics defeated the Soviet Union, 3-2, in the semifinals at Lake Placid, N.Y. The game was dubbed "The Miracle on Ice" and cemented Eruzione's place as one of America's greatest sports heroes.

The United States captured the final to win the gold medal, its first in the Olympics since 1960 at Squaw Valley, California.

Eruzione, who was a three-sport athlete at Winthrop and captain of the hockey team at Boston University, was not a big scorer, but he was the U.S. captain and the emotional leader of the team.

Many of Eruzione's Olympic teammates turned professional, but Eruzione realized a pro career wasn't in the offing, and he became a broadcaster.

A few weeks before the Globe banquet, Eruzione and I met for lunch at a Winthrop restaurant to go over the particulars of his speech.

Eruzione is a very grounded and down-to-earth person who never expected to be a celebrity and, despite the fame he achieved, was having difficulty being a celebrity.

"It's great that we won the gold medal, but there is a downside to being a celebrity," Eruzione told me. "I now play in a number of celebrity golf tournaments. It's supposed to be a fun time, but a lot of time the other golfers try too hard to beat me so they can say they beat an Olympic gold medal winner."

He even had to stop playing in a no-check hockey league because he was being checked all over the ice.

Eruzione had just completed his first season as a color commentator on New York Rangers hockey broadcasts. "I enjoyed it very much, but it was a grind," he said.

For each game, Eruzione was picked up by a limousine at his Winthrop home and was driven to close-by Logan Airport for the short plane ride to LaGuardia Airport, where another limousine drove him to Madison Square Garden.

After the game, Eruzione took a limousine to the airport, where he took the last flight of the day back to Boston, and then had his final limousine ride of the day back to his home.

Eruzione was well received by the Globe's All-Scholastic

audience after his stirring speech recalling his wonderful Olympic experience.

****

I'll never forget the quest for the 1989 All-Scholastic banquet speaker.

Twice, we had legendary Penn State football coach Joe Paterno lined up as the banquet speaker, and twice circumstances forced Paterno to back out.

Paterno assured me he fully intended to be our 1989 banquet speaker, but my phone rang a few weeks before the banquet, and it was Paterno.

"I'm sorry, Larry, but the athletic department advised me new recruiting rules prevent me from speaking certain times a year when underclassmen are going to be present," he said.

I thanked Paterno for the call and began a search for a replacement. It was hard enough to find speakers, let alone having to restart the task three weeks before the banquet.

I made dozens of unsuccessful calls trying to secure a speaker, but I hit pay dirt when I called my cousin, George Small, a vice-president at Franklin Sporting Goods.

I asked him if he could recommend anyone from the company's stable of athletes, and he came up with boxer Roy Jones Jr., the U.S. Olympic boxer who had been robbed of a gold medal at the 1988 Summer Olympics at Seoul, Korea.

The decision had been universally condemned because Jones had dominated each of the rounds, and even the declared victor in the fight came over to Jones to apologize for the judges' decision.

After speaking with Jones' father, his manager, an agreement was made to fly Jones Jr. to Boston from Pensacola and to house him at the Copley Marriott for the weekend.

I thought my problems were over, but they were, in fact, just beginning.

A few days later, Roy Jones Sr. called me. "I'm concerned about security. I'm sending two bodyguards with Roy Jr.," he told me. Boxed into a corner, I agreed, as the cost of two more round-trip flights were added to the tab, but I didn't have much choice. My wife, Bunny, and I picked up Jones and his two bodyguards at Logan Airport on a late Friday afternoon, two days before the banquet.

I spotted Jones at the gate. How could I have missed him? He was sporting an oversized Mexican sombrero and was wearing a hugely decorative Korean jacket, the type American soldiers brought back after the Korean Conflict in the 1950s.

We took the threesome to a restaurant for dinner and then registered them into the Copley Marriott, where my wife and I were staying for the All-Scholastic weekend.

Within an hour of Jones' checking in, I received a call from his father in Pensacola.

"Roy isn't happy with his room. We were expecting a suite," he said.

I told him, "Roy was in a very nice corner room with plenty of space. Plus, the hotel is sold out."

Early the next morning, I received a call from the Marriott front desk. "Mr. Jones ordered hundreds of dollars of food from room service last night. Was that all right?"

I assured the caller The Globe would pay for it. Two hours later, Jones called me. "I need my suit pressed," he said.

Finding a cleaner doing pressing work in downtown Boston on a Saturday proved to be a near impossible task. I finally reached a cleaner in South Boston who would do the work. I took Jones' suit to the cleaner and waited for him to press it.

My next chore for the Jones entourage was a tour of Boston. Jones was bored, so Bunny and I took Jones and his bodyguards on a two-hour tour of the city.

My anxiety level on Sunday afternoon, the day of the banquet, was high.

I didn't have many expectations for a twenty-one-year-old speaker, but I was wrong. Jones wooed the crowd with a stirring speech.

When I drove Jones and his body guards back to Logan Airport on Monday morning, I was relieved that my adventure was over. There is an incredible number of details involved in pulling off a 1,500-person banquet, and I had added celebrity escort to that list.

Jones went on to become one of the great boxers of the 1990s and 2000s, winning multiple world titles in several weight classes.

****

Over the course of the sixteen years I worked as assistant sports editor/schools at The Globe, we added eleven All-Scholastic teams to the existing twenty-five. We expanded All-Scholastic coverage to the private and prep schools and added a program for Central Massachusetts.

The addition of which I am proudest is The Globe All-Scholastic Academic team. I had approached management at The Globe in 1985, asking approval for a $12,000 expenditure for the program, which would honor six boys and six girls with $1,000 scholarships starting in the 1986-87 school year.

I appeared before a management committee, headed by Globe president John Giuggio, to make my pitch. I was confident in my presentation, and I was rewarded with approval. The Globe's management was always extremely community conscious, and along with the All-Scholastic program, the paper sponsored the State Drama Festival and the State Science Fair. The Globe Foundation also annually donated $5 million to worthy charities in Massachusetts.

We broke the Eastern Mass. region into six areas. Schools were allowed to nominate one boy and one girl.

We organized a selection committee consisting of coaches, athletic directors, principals, superintendents of schools, and school committee members.

I wanted our Globe All-Scholastic speaker in 1987 to be someone who would be academically connected to our inaugural All-Scholastic Academic Team.

I immediately thought of tennis great Arthur Ashe, whose image and prestige among world athletes was impeccable.

Ashe had risen from the tennis courts of Richmond, Va., to become an internationally recognized leader.

I called ProServe, the agency that most world tennis players used, and asked Ashe's fee for speaking.

My jaw dropped when I was told it was $10,000. Our speaking fee at that time was $2,000, but I was not surprised to hear of Ashe's asking price.

Not to be dismayed, I had a secret weapon.

I called Globe tennis correspondent Bud Collins, perhaps the preeminent tennis writer in the world. Bud had been a full-time Globe employee, but NBC lured him away in the late seventies to handle interviews at the Grand Slam tennis tournaments. Collins still covered the Grand Slam events for The Globe and many other tennis events as well.

I told Collins of my predicament, and I asked him if he could obtain Ashe's services as The Globe All-Scholastic speaker.

Two weeks later, my phone rang. "Hi, this is Arthur Ashe, and I am your speaker."

We asked our speakers to keep their remarks to twenty minutes because we didn't want our banquet to run too long.

Ashe's speech was inspiring, and as he concluded his forty-five minute talk, he received a rousing ovation.

As he sat down next to me, he whispered, "Was I too long?"

"No," I responded. "You were perfect."

The Day Larry Bird Retired

The 1992 Barcelona Olympics was one of the most anticipated in memory, and The Globe had its usual large cast of writers, editors, and photographers on hand to cover the competition.

So when the Olympics concluded, the Globe contingent returned to Boston, and headed by sports Editor Don Skwar, went on vacation.

My responsibility, as one of the assistant sports editors, was to be the day sports editor for two weeks.

It was expected to be a very quiet time. Besides Red Sox coverage, there was very little going on in the area.

On the morning of August 18, 1992, I arrived at the office to prepare for the morning briefing by department heads.

Shortly before the meeting, word came that Larry Bird, the Celtics legend, was retiring.

Top level Globe brass gathered to decide what to do. A call to Converse, one of the companies Bird endorsed, produced a full page ad which served to pay for the newsprint for what would become an eight-page special section for the next morning's newspaper.

The only decision remaining was the size of the press run. The Globe sold in excess of 520,000 papers for the daily, and I recommended that we increase the press run by 10 percent.

My suggestion was dismissed because, it was pointed out, that special editions for breaking news, rarely increase circulation by five percent.

I argued that because of Bird's popularity a special section would boost street sales, and because many subscribers would be on vacation in August, many would want back copies. A Bird special section would result in additional sales from memorabilia buffs.

A decision was made to increase the morning press run by five percent.

Skwar was called and made aware of the situation, and he said he would immediately drive to the Globe office from his Cape Cod cottage.

The biggest obstacle to producing the special section was the lack of staff to write the content for the eight-page section. Different staff members were assigned to find the vacationing writers and columnists who covered the Celtics regularly.

I was assigned to find Jackie MacMullan, the Celtics beat writer. It became a Herculean task, partly because cell phones were not commonplace, and partly because the writers did not want to be disturbed, particularly after the rigors of covering an Olympics.

I made calls to Jackie's parents and the parents of her husband, Michael. I called the alumni office of the University of New Hampshire, where she played college basketball, and to many other friends and sources.

After a long stretch of fruitless calls, I was able to find out that Jackie and her husband were at a cottage on a lake somewhere in New Hampshire.

The next round of calls was made to every campground in New Hampshire. After a few hours of calls, I succeeded in finding Jackie's location, only to have the manager tell me that he just saw her drive away.

I asked if he would relay a message to Jackie and her husband when they returned and to tell her it was vital that she call the office at once.

When they returned later that afternoon, the manager told her of my message, and Jackie called the office.

She immediately drove back to Boston and wrote the lead story for the special section.

I joined the copy desk that night to help in the editing process, and I spent the rest of the night in the composing room making up the special section.

I left the paper at 1:30 a.m., quite exhausted but quite satisfied after completing one of the most interesting work days ever.

However, I was disappointed that Globe management had rejected my call for a ten percent boost in the press run.

As I had expected, street sales for the morning paper with the Larry Bird special section were brisk. In fact, the paper experienced a rarity—a sold out edition.

Because of demand for the special section, the Globe ran off another 30,000 copies in an extra press run.

Even with strong sales of the special section, the added press run was made on overtime, and the paper actually lost money on the additional papers.

It was the only time that I had been involved in a high-level decision, and the fact that I had been right but had been overruled didn't diminish the thrill of the day's events.

A Private Audience With DePaul Legend Ray Meyer

Brockton High basketball standout Curtis Jackson was recruited to play basketball at DePaul University after his graduation in 1986, but he was ineligible to play as a freshman because he failed to meet Proposition 48 academic standards.

I had heard from Brockton basketball coach Vic Ortiz that Jackson was doing well in his first semester at DePaul. I decided to head to Chicago and see how Jackson was adjusting to college academic life and how he felt about sitting out his freshman year.

At the start of his second semester at DePaul, I found Jackson adjusting to college life quite well. He had a 3.0 average (equal to a B grade) in his first semester, majoring in communications with a minor in business.

DePaul enrolled Jackson in a "bridge program" over the summer to acquaint him to college life. The college continued to monitor Jackson through the office of academic adviser Shirley Tompkins, who regularly met with Jackson and checked his progress with his instructors and tutors.

"I don't know if I could have done it alone, especially at the beginning," said Jackson. "It was difficult at the beginning when we had the intrasquad and exhibition games."

But Jackson was philosophical. "I have grown a lot; I'm hungry now," he said. "The experience was positive, and it made me hungry to prove myself."

While waiting to speak with DePaul basketball coach Joey Meyer, I had the opportunity and privilege to meet Meyer's father, Ray, the legendary DePaul coach who had compiled a 724-354 record from 1942 to 1984.

Since his retirement, Meyer had become an assistant to the DePaul president, making speeches and attending numerous breakfast, lunch, and dinner meetings throughout Chicago and around the country.

I was spellbound by Meyer's enthusiasm and energy as he spoke of his job as the college's goodwill ambassador.

Meyer told me a story about Chicago quarterback Jim McMahon, who had led the Bears to a Super Bowl victory over the New England Patriots.

"McMahon was offered $5,000 to appear before a group, but he declined because it was his wedding anniversary. Undaunted, the group increased the offer to $10,000, but the answer was still the same. The offer was raised to $20,000, and McMahon finally caved in. 'My wife can wait,' was his response."

I'm not sure Meyer's story was true, but like the many yarns and stories he told me in the forty-five minutes we spent together, I thoroughly enjoyed being entertained by one of the most interesting characters I had ever met.

Meanwhile, Curtis Jackson, the young man DePaul accepted as a Prop. 48 student, played basketball for the university and graduated with a degree in communications and marketing.

He played basketball professionally in South America, Puerto Rico, Dominican Republic, Europe, and China.

He operates Jackson Financial Systems, specializing in retirement income planning and insurance.

When Jackson graduated from college, I invited him to be among the speakers at The Globe All-Scholastic banquet.

A Rookie's First Pro Interview

In 1975, a year after I joined *The Salem News* staff, I occasionally covered New England Patriots games.

I often attended the weekly Wednesday practices when Sunday's opposing coach would be on a conference call. That allowed me to write an advance for Sunday's games with information from the Patriots' opponents.

I also interviewed a Patriots player and wrote a feature story for Saturday's paper.

After Week 5 of the season, the Patriots were on their second quarterback of the season. Coach Chuck Fairbanks had replaced No. 1 quarterback Jim Plunkett after he posted a 2-3 record, with backup Neil Graf, who proceeded to lose his debut.

When I went to Foxborough on the following Wednesday, I was assigned to speak to Graf and do a feature on how he felt about replacing Plunkett, a former Heisman Trophy winner.

The Patriots' policy on player interviews during midweek practices in 1975 was to make a request to the public relations staff. After the weekly conference call, I asked Patriots pubic relations spokesman Denny Lynch if I could speak with Graf.

He returned shortly without Graf. "Neil doesn't want to speak," he told me.

"Gee, Denny, I need to speak with someone for my feature," I said.

Lynch went down to the locker room and brought up the third string quarterback who was now Graf's backup.

I asked him how he was enjoying his rookie season in the NFL, and was surprised at his answer.

"I'm not really having a good time in the pros. In training camp, I didn't get any reps, and no one would stay after practice to work with me. This isn't what I expected," he said.

He went on to list a number of complaints he had with his NFL experience, which made for an unusual interview, his first as a pro.

A week later, after Graf lost his second game, the rookie from Kansas State, drafted 116th overall in the fifth round, became the Patriots' starting quarterback.

My interview with Steve Grogan the previous week, was the first of many he would have as quarterback for the Patriots from 1975 to 1990. When he retired, Grogan would have thrown for 182 touchdowns and 26,886 yards in the NFL.

Alone On The Expressway

Aside from the lengthy hours at work, getting there was often a major task during the winter months.

When I awakened at 4:45 the morning of February 7, 1978, at my West Peabody home, I was expecting a lot of snow.

The Blizzard of '78, as it was so labeled, had begun the afternoon before, and the temperature had plummeted more than 40 degrees in a few hours.

We had lost our heat, but that was the least of our problems as my wife and I headed into the living room. We looked out the front window of the house and saw that snow had totally covered our front door.

When we opened our garage door, we gazed at our driveway, which was covered by fifty inches of snow. There was no way our snowblower could operate with more than four feet of snow on the ground.

Ironically, grass was visible on the front yard of our neighbor's house across the street, owing to the weird wind pattern of the Nor'easter.

I called my boss, *Salem News* Sports Editor Bill Kipouras, to tell him I wouldn't be making it into the office today.

"What do you mean you won't be at work today?" he shouted. "It's not that bad in downtown Peabody."

"Well, we have 50 inches of snow in our driveway," I responded.

Massachusetts Gov. Michael Dukakis called a state of emergency that day and ordered all cars off the road for a week. Police, fire, hospital, and emergency personnel were allowed on the roads. Newspaper employees were exempt, too, since the governor felt it was important for people being at home to have a newspaper to avoid cabin fever.

My paper did publish the next morning. It included a story exempting newspaper personnel from the car ban.

After shoveling our driveway during the day, I placed the newspaper story in my glove compartment, in case I was stopped while driving to work the next morning.

I'm glad I did. The following morning, I headed to work, which took a significant amount of time since I was stopped seven times during my seven-mile drive to work. Each time I showed the exemption story to a police officer or National Guardsman.

We had called our oil company service department to report our furnace breakdown, and were promised someone would come out "whenever possible."

Fortunately, our wait was only two days, but our house was not cold since the snow blowing off the reservoir down the street from our house, formed a wall of snow right up to our roof.

On Saturday morning, we were running out of staples, and we needed to go to the supermarket, more than a mile from our house.

"Since you have the exemption, do you think we can take the car to the market?" my wife asked.

"Not in a thousand years," I said. "We'll walk like everyone else."

So we walked to the store, along with hundreds of our West Peabody neighbors and hundreds more from neighboring Lynnfield, which did not have a supermarket in town.

Early that afternoon, I left the house and headed to Boston, where I was trying out for a position on The Boston Globe sports copy desk. The trial had started the previous October and ended with my being hired in June.

As I started my drive into Boston, there were still vehicles clearing snow, several days after the blizzard. Heading over the Mystic River Bridge and onto the Southeast Expressway, I looked around, but I didn't see another vehicle on the road.

Here I was in downtown Boston, and I was alone on a road that carried more than 160,000 vehicles a day. I never remember being in an eerier position.

Arriving Home From Fenway At 2 A.M.

I was a pretty responsible youngster growing up in the Dorchester section of Boston. My mother usually gave me a lot of latitude when it came to going into the city to watch the Red Sox, Celtics, and Bruins.

But on the night of May 12, 1959, as a fourteen-year-old ninth grader, I feared I would never be allowed to see another sporting event for the rest of my life.

I somehow convinced my mother to allow me to go to the Red Sox-White Sox Tuesday night home game at Fenway Park. She questioned my judgment, but I promised her I would be home at a reasonable time, and she relented.

It was a terrific game that was tied at 2 after nine innings. I thought about leaving, but an announcement told the crowd that all trains and buses would still be running when the game ended, so I decided to stay.

The game dragged into the 12th inning, and I was still there.

In the top of the 12th, Al Smith hit a two-run homer over the wall in left field off Murray Wall to give the White Sox a 4-2 lead. Wall had kept the White Sox without a run in his four previous innings.

I should have left at that point, but I didn't.

In the bottom of the 12th inning, Ted Williams grounded out to second and Frank Malzone popped up to second. Once again I debated leaving.

But Jackie Jensen hit a solo home run to bring the Red Sox within a run, and I decided to wait until the game ended.

Dick Gernert reached on an error, and up came catcher Sammy White, who was 0-for-5 at that point. White hung in bravely, fouling off pitch after pitch. As White softly flied out to left to end the four hour, twenty-three-minute game, I bolted for the exit.

I ran to the Kenmore station, but because many of the crowd of 22,000 had beaten me to the subway station, it took a while before I was aboard a train that took me to Park St.

I once again had to wait until another train came along, and I rode that train one stop to Washington St. There I boarded another train that took me to my final subway stop, Egelston Square.

I raced down the stairs to catch the trackless trolley that would take me home via Blue Hill Avenue, only to gaze at the trolley exiting the station.

Here I was, at 1 a.m., stranded, with no further trolleys scheduled until 5:30 a.m.

I found a pay phone and called home.

Needless to say, my mother was less than thrilled, but she was happy I was safe.

She dressed and drove to Egelston Square, retrieving me from my long escapade.

When we arrived home, it was 2 a.m.

It was the last time for a while that I would be going to Fenway at night.

At The Birth Of A Football League

Little did I realize when I headed to Boston University's Nickerson Field on the night of September 9, 1960, that I was going to attend a historic football game.

The Friday game between the Boston Patriots and the Denver Broncos was the first in the history of the American Football League and was the first professional football game in Boston since the Redskins left in 1939 and headed to Washington. There was little hope that the league would survive, considering it was striving to become a rival to the powerful National Football League.

The entry fee for an AFL franchise was a meager $25,000, considerably less than the $125,000 the Boston Red Sox paid future Hall of Famer Ted Williams in his final season.

There were few takers for the $25,000 fee because it was generally believed the new football league wouldn't last long.

Billy Sullivan, the Boston Patriots' owner, scheduled Friday night home games because he didn't want to go head-to-head with NFL games scheduled for Sunday afternoons.

Sullivan, a former Boston Braves publicist, chose Nickerson Field and its expanded 21,000 seat stadium for the Patriots' first home field.

Three weeks before my sixteenth birthday, I paid $2.50 for my ticket in the end zone to see the game. I resisted paying $5 for an expensive box seat. That represented nearly seven hours of wages I earned as a stock boy at a Dorchester women's clothing store after school.

I was among 21,597 fans who welcomed the Patriots and the AFL for the inaugural game. Unfortunately, Denver, a 16-point underdog, spoiled Boston's home opener with a 13-10 victory, thanks to a 76-yard punt return by Denver's Gene Mingo in the third period.

I attended a number of Patriots' games over the years, in venues such as Harvard, Fenway Park, and Foxborough, but the opening game at BU remained my favorite because it was the night the AFL took off. In the September 10, 2010 issue of Sports illustrated, Dick Friedman, an SI writer and copy editor, wrote a story of the first game in AFL history to commemorate the fiftieth anniversary of the league.

I had met Friedman at the *Sports Illustrated* offices in New York in December 1998, when I visited a former Boston Globe co-op, B.J. Schecter, a standout editor at SI.

When I read Friedman's story on the first AFL game, I e-mailed Schecter and asked him to relay my congratulations to Friedman on a job well done.

Friedman mentioned in the story that he had attended the game with another 9-year-old from Newton, Chris Henes.

Interestingly, I also knew Henes. During my time at *The News-Tribune* in Waltham, I had covered many high school games at Newton South High, where Henes was a manager of sports teams. I had called on Henes to provide statistics for game stories and features.

Schecter had passed along my best wishes to Friedman, who started a back-and-forth e-mail correspondence with me about that first AFL game.

In his final e-mail, Friedman revealed that there had been one other 9-year-old from Newton attending his first pro football game that night.

"I tried to reach him to include his recollection of the game, but he was busy preparing for the NFL season," Friedman e-mailed me.

The name of that nine year old?

Jeff Lurie, owner of the Philadelphia Eagles.

Responsible For An International Incident

In the six years I worked part time for *The Boston Herald*, I often covered events such as yachting, equestrian competitions, dog shows, and polo and rugby matches.

It was quite a challenge for a city kid whose family lived in apartments with no back yards. "The only grass I ever saw was the weeds coming up through the cracks in the sidewalk," I often joked.

Several novice reporters and I were fortunate to lean on Boston Globe yachting writer John Ahern, a city alumnus as well, for advice. When covering the equestrian and dog shows, I always managed to find a New York Times reporter to learn what was going on.

By the time I joined the staff of *The Salem News* in 1974, I was able to cover the yachting scene off Marblehead and the equestrian and polo activities in Hamilton.

So when it was announced that British Princess Anne and her husband, Capt. Mark Phillips, would be part of a British equestrian team competing in an international competition in Nell Ayer's Ledyard Farm in 1977, the paper planned extensive coverage. On a hot day in July, I met with Ayer, a prominent Boston businessman and president of the board of directors of Beverly Hospital, at his estate's party barn in Wenham to begin accumulating information about the competition.

In the course of our three-hour meeting, I inquired if it would be possible to have the princess and the rest of the British team be part of a pre-competition news conference.

Ayer said he wasn't sure it was possible, but he would check into it.

A week later, with conditions approved, a news conference was scheduled a couple of days before the competition started. One condition of the news conference was that questions would be posed to all members of the British team, not just to the princess and her husband.

Because of security concerns, all media would need to apply for credentials. A gathering point was set, so all media members could be transported to Ayer's party barn for the news conference.

The first couple of questions were about the competition, but the third question, posed by Boston Globe columnist Jeremiah Murphy, was a bombshell.

Addressing the princess, Murphy asked, "How does it feel to be a quirk of nature?" (that is, to be born to the Queen of England).

Princess Anne, obviously taken aback, responded, "Do I have horns?"

The news conference was abruptly ended as I stood there in complete shock. After all, this news conference was my idea, and it couldn't have ended any worse.

Later in the day, I learned that this was the first news conference for a member of British royalty, and, I was sure, it would be the last.

When I got home, my wife asked me how it had gone. "I am responsible for creating an international incident," I said.

Harvard Wasn't A Friend

Because the state facility that high school track athletes in Massachusetts used to practice and run in meets was demolished in 1958 to make way for an extension of the Mass. Turnpike into Boston, the state athletic association was forced to use the track at Harvard for its major meets.

One year, I received a call from Bob McIntyre, the president of the state track coaches association. He told me that Harvard was planning a gigantic increase in the rental fee for the track and that the fee increase was unaffordable.

I told him I would take care of it.

After considerable thought, I came up with the solution.

I would write a Sunday column blasting the rental boost.

My argument would be that Harvard was a tax exempt institution and charging so much for a rental would constitute making a profit. Therefore, Harvard should have its tax exempt status removed by the legislature.

Before I wrote the column, I decided to throw my idea out to Speaker of the Massachusetts Legislature, Charles Flaherty, Democrat from Cambridge.

I called Flaherty, told him of the situation, and asked what he thought of my idea.

His response: "Sounds all right with me, Larry."

So I wrote the column for that Sunday.

On Tuesday morning, I received a call from McIntyre telling me that the rental fee increase had been rescinded. Harvard had backed down.

I pushed for the building of a new state track facility for eleven years. Finally, in 1993, with Flaherty's help, the legislature passed a bill that was approved. The new indoor track opened in 1995 and celebrated its twentieth anniversary with a gala in October 2015, where I was honored with a "Persistence Award."

Thankfully, we didn't need our "friends" at Harvard anymore.

Having Lunch With JoJo Starbuck

In today's crowded field of sports, it's hard to believe that in the decade of the 1970s, the Ice Capades was considered an event worthy of coverage.

But its annual visit to Boston Garden was deemed newsworthy, and I was assigned to cover the news conference and luncheon previewing the 1973 Ice Capades.

The news conference didn't produce much newsworthy, but I lucked out when JoJo Starbuck, the show's headliner, sat next to me at the luncheon.

Starbuck, the 1972 U.S. Olympian and four-time United States champion, had joined the Ice Capades the year before.

I was more interested in learning what it was like to be a member of the Ice Capades than hearing about the details of the show itself, so I asked Starbuck about the daily rigors of being a star with the Ice Capades.

I expected to hear that it was a glamorous and exciting gig, but I found out otherwise.

"We have a very rigorous schedule," said Starbuck. "The day starts early, and we go full tilt all day.

"On show days, we have to attend dance class, and we practice before every show. We have to watch our diet because we have to maintain a certain weight."

The schedule, Starbuck noted, is particularly hard on weekends where there are matinee performances on Saturdays and Sundays in addition to evening performances.

"On Mondays, we head off to the next town, and repeat the schedule," she said.

In many respects, an Ice Capades performer has a tougher life than most professional athletes.

Held Prisoner By Shula

On December 12, 1982, in one of the most controversial plays in National Football League history, Mark Henderson, an inmate at a nearby prison to Schaefer Stadium, cleared a spot on a snowy field, allowing New England Patriots kicker John Smith to kick a 33-yard field goal that gave the Patriots a 3-0 victory over the Miami Dolphins.

Miami coach Don Shula protested, but the field goal was ruled good.

Shula met with NFL Commissioner Pete Rozelle several days later, and although Rozelle agreed with Shula that the use of the plow gave the Patriots an unfair advantage, he said that he had never reversed the result of a game and was not going to start doing so.

The defeat was devastating to the Dolphins, who lost the top seed in the AFC playoffs to the Oakland Raiders.

When the first-round playoff pairings were announced, the Dolphins were handed a huge chance for revenge by drawing the Patriots as their opponent in the game that was immediately dubbed Revenge of the Snowplow in the Orange Bowl.

To this day, Shula still fumes about the Snowplow game, but as the playoff game against the Patriots neared, he advised his public relations staff to make sure visiting media didn't ask him about it because he didn't want it to become the focal point of the game.

"What's happened is gone, over, and done. We have to get ready for a whole new game with New England. What happened is not popular with me or with the players," said Shula. "The incentive to win this game isn't to atone for the 3-0 loss. It's to make sure we're still in the playoffs next week. It's just a coincidence our next game is against New England."

Because I was heading to Florida early that week to visit my mother, I volunteered to cover the Dolphins' Wednesday media session and file a notebook for Thursday's Globe.

It's rare for an out-of-town writer to show up for a practice at an opponent's midweek news conference, so I called veteran Dolphins public relations director Harvey Greene to alert him off my intentions to be at the Dolphins' training center in Davie.

When I arrived, Greene pulled me aside.

"The Dolphins' beat writers and columnists are not allowed at closed practices, and they usually wait in the press room, but coach Shula is sensitive about an out-of-town media member being in the complex, so we're going to put you in a private room and keep the door closed," Greene said.

After the practice, Shula was genial, and I was able to get the material I needed.

I'd been through a number of unusual circumstances as a member of the visiting press before, but I'd never been held a prisoner.

Helping The Stewart Family During A Difficult Time

There are times as a journalist when you have to step out of your role as a reporter and editor and become a friend and helper.

Such was the case on December 6, 1987, when I, as a friend of legendary Boston coach Bill Stewart Jr. and his family, helped during a difficult time.

I had just arrived at my desk at The Globe, beginning to prepare to work on my weekly high school sports pages, when my phone rang. "Hi, Larry, this is Bill Stewart, calling to tell you that dad died this morning."

Bill Stewart Jr. was, perhaps, the most legendary coach in Boston scholastic sports history, guiding the Boston English High football, hockey, and baseball teams for more than three and a half decades. His father was the legendary major league baseball umpire, Bill Stewart Sr., and all the younger Stewarts officiated in football, hockey and baseball.

In fact, in Bill Stewart's 400th victory as Boston English's baseball coach, his son, Bill Stewart III, umpired at home, son Paul officiated at first, and son James umpired at third. Grandson Gilbert was the catcher for the opposing team, Groton School.

I informed the news desk of Stewart's death, and we agreed that I would write the obituary. I took great pride in the obituaries and appreciations I wrote because, in almost all the cases, I knew the deceased well, as did a large segment of our readership.

I made a number of calls over the next few hours and wrote the obituary which was to run the next morning.

When I finished the obituary, I began to work on my high school pages when my phone rang again. It was Bill Stewart III calling back with a request.

"Larry, we need your help," he said. "Paul is officiating tonight, and we don't know where he is. Can you help us locate him? If you find him, don't tell him the news, but just ask that he call home."

I promised Stewart I would help out, but I had no idea how I would pursue it. Paul was in his first year as a National Hockey League official, but locating the place where an official might be is almost impossible since leagues keep such information a secret. I called Boston Bruins beat writer Fran Rosa at home and asked how I might pursue the search. Rosa was familiar with Bill Stewart since he covered high school sports when he was a young reporter at The Globe.

"I happened to be speaking with the head of officials last night, and he told me that Paul was officiating in Edmonton," said Rosa.

I looked up the phone number for the Edmonton Coliseum, but held out little hope that an operator would answer the phone on a Sunday night. I fully expected to get a recording.

To my surprise, an operator answered the call. I explained the situation to the operator and asked if I could speak to Oilers public relations director Bill Tuele.

She connected me to the press box shortly before the game was scheduled to start.

I told Tuele that referee Paul Stewart's father had died and that the family wanted to speak with him. He agreed to speak with Paul after the game and said he would not give him the details, but just ask that he call home.

I called Bill Stewart III. I told him I had found Paul and that he would call home after the game.

I attended Bill Stewart's wake two days later in Milton, sad that a friend had died, but glad I was able to help the family.

Interviewing Gene Sarazen, Knickers And All

When the Francis Ouimet Scholarship Fund was established in 1968, organizers wanted a prominent name to headline a special exhibition prior to the start of the inaugural Ouimet Memorial Tournament at Woodland Golf Club in Auburndale, Mass.

Answering the call was Hall of Fame golfer Gene Sarazen, a longtime friend of Ouimet. Sarazen's presence was a major boost to the tournament and the fund, which has provided scholarships to caddies from tournament proceeds. The tournament will turn fifty in 2018.

Ouimet, who died in 1967, was a prominent golfer who shocked the golf world in 1913. As a twenty-year-old, he defeated renowned British golfers Harry Vardon and Ted Ray to win the U.S. Open at The Country Club in Brookline, Mass.

Ouimet and Sarazen started golfing when they were caddies and went on to distinguished careers in golf. Ouimet was a member at Woodland and played most of his golf on the course.

Sarazen, who died in 1999 at age ninety-seven, was considered one of the top golfers of the twentieth century. His double eagle 2 on the 15th hole at Augusta National Golf Club is considered one of golf's greatest shots and led him to the Masters championship, one of his forty-eight tour wins. Sarazen, Bobby Jones, and Walter Hagen were considered the most dominant golfers in the 1920s and into the 1930s.

While at The *News-Tribune in* Waltham, I spent a lot of time during the year at Woodland. Tom Murphy, The News-Tribune's managing editor, was a member at Woodland, and I covered any major event at Woodland, including the member-guest tournaments, the New England Senior championships, and the high school girls' state golf championship.

Murphy was able to get me a private interview with Sarazen the day before the exhibition.

Although only five feet five inches tall, Sarazen was an imposing figure. Dressed nattily with his trademark knickers. He was true to his reputation as an outspoken personality.

We talked about a number of golf subjects, but Sarazen was most boisterous about the pace of golfers.

"The pro golfers today take way too much time on the course, consulting with caddies on every shot and putt," said Sarazen, who spent only a few seconds before hitting his drive or putting.

I told Sarazen that I admired his support for the inaugural Ouimet tournament. "Francis and I were great friends, and we started golf as caddies. It's important for me to be here to honor my friend and help establish a fund to help caddies along the way," he said.

I followed Sarazen around the course during the special exhibition. It was a great thrill for me to have met and interviewed one of golf's great names.

Pete Rose At His Height
And At His Nadir

Although self created, one of the saddest sagas in the history of baseball is the banishment of Cincinnati Reds great Pete Rose.

Rose starred for the Cincinnati teams that won back-to-back World Series championships in 1975 and '76, and set an NL record with a 44-game hitting streak in 1978.

After signing with the Philadelphia Phillies as a free agent, he helped them win a World Series in 1980.

Rose spent half of a season with the Montreal Expos in 1984, then returned to Cincinnati as player-manager. On September 11, 1985, he recorded career hit No. 4,192 to break the fifty-seven-year-old record held by baseball great Ty Cobb.

Rose ended his playing career after the 1986 season with 4,256 total hits, and held the all-time records with 3,562 games played and 14,053 at-bats.

Rose continued to serve as manager of the Reds, but after suspicions arose about his gambling habits, the Commissioner's office hired former Justice Department prosecutor John Dowd to launch an investigation. Dowd uncovered evidence that Rose had bet on baseball games, and on August 23, 1989, Commissioner Bart Giamatti suspended Rose from baseball for life.

Rose ran afoul of the law the following year, earning a five-month sentence in a Federal correctional institution for tax evasion.

Rose applied for reinstatement to baseball in 1997, and after years of denying the charges, he finally admitted to betting on games in 2004.

I interviewed Rose three times in his career. The first time was after Games 6 and 7 of the 1975 World Series. The '75 World Series was one of Rose's great moments in baseball.

The next two times I spoke with Rose was post banishment and, obviously, a difficult time.

After Carlton Fisk's 12th inning home run had given the Boston Red Sox a 7-6 victory in Game 6 and a 3-3 tie in the 1975 World Series, Rose was hardly despondent in the Reds' locker room.

"It was a privilege to play in this game. I believe this is the best played game in the history of the World Series," said Rose.

In 1995, I came across Rose once again. This time he was playing in an unsanctioned old-timers game in Phoenix.

Rose was his candid and outspoken self as I interviewed him before the game. I asked him if he still felt that game 6 of the 1975 World Series was the best World Series game in history.

"Definitely," he said. 'It was such a joy and pleasure just to be part of that game."

Earlier in '95, baseball had voted for expansion for the 1998 season, and Rose was not a big supporter of expansion.

"There aren't enough pitchers of major league caliber now. It will be worse in 1998," he said. "The batting averages and home runs will be out of sight," Rose predicted.

As it turns out, Rose was correct. The 1998 season marked the home run battle between Mark McGwire and Sammy

Sosa, although the home run competition between McGwire and Sosa that season was diminished because of suspected steroid use.

The last time I saw Rose was in 2000 when I covered Sparky Anderson's induction into baseball's Hall of Fame.

He had a stand on Main St. in Cooperstown, selling autographs, which has been his major source of income since his banishment.

Rose's banishment and ineligibility for the Hall of Fame was heightened that year when two Cincinnati players, Anderson and broadcaster Marty Brenneman were inducted.

Had he followed baseball's rules and had not bet on baseball, Rose would have been a major part of the Cincinnati-dominated festivities.

Many argue that Pete Rose deserves to be in the Hall of Fame. There is an argument that Ty Cobb was a nasty person but is still in the Hall of Fame.

Whether Rose ever does gain entry to the Hall is a matter of conjecture, but his action off the field will forever tarnish his accomplishments on the field.

Success In One Day Vs. Eleven Years

Writing a column brings with it a huge responsibility.

While the words and the opinions are yours, there are tremendous journalistic and other responsibilities that go hand in hand with penning an opinion piece.

Research and knowledge are important attributes to a column, but the opinions expressed are yours, and I always felt the need to justify a column before I wrote it.

During the eleven years I battled to get a state track facility built in Boston, I always wondered how each of the columns would be received.

One column I wrote for the *Ventura County Star* in California netted a result in twenty-four hours.

When we decided to run a front-page feature on the planned athletic expansion at Cal Lutheran University in Thousand Oaks, California, I wondered if it would be the best time to write a column suggesting the college create a home for the Ventura County Sports Hall of Fame.

The Star had been a proud sponsor of the Ventura County Sports Hall of Fame for a number of years, but when I joined the paper, the relationship needed some attention.

Star Publisher Tim Gallagher knew of my commitment to community involvement, and he called me into his office to discuss the relationship between the newspaper and the Hall of Fame.

He asked me if I would meet with the Hall of Fame leaders to try to mend the relationship.

I attended a few meetings with the leadership of the Hall of Fame to get to know them and their mission.

One ongoing issue was finding a home for all the permanent plaques that were handed out to inductees every year. I learned that The Star had been storing the plaques in its basement, and once a year, they were brought to the Hall of Fame dinner.

When Cal Lutheran University Vice President of Marketing and Communications Ritch Eich and Vice President of administration Steve Wheatley came to The Star to discuss the planned expansion of the athletic facilities at Cal Lutheran, I was invited to join the meeting.

Part of the discussion dealt with the college's desires to become more integrated into the Ventura County community.

One of my suggestions to Eich and Wheatley was to have the college invite the community to utilize some of its planned facilities for meets and tournaments. That way more people would become more aware of the college.

We assigned David Lassen, who had covered Cal Lutheran sports for a long time, to do an extensive story on the university's athletic plans.

Lassen's story started out on the front page of the Sunday paper and jumped to a full page inside. The feature included a large graphic detailing all of the college's future buildings and fields. I added a column which suggested that the college might create more interest from the community if it became the permanent home of the Ventura County Sports Hall of Fame.

Lassen did an excellent job of outlining the college's plans, and I was pleased with the package we had presented our readers.

I was concerned that the college might have felt that I was telling them what to do, always a dangerous practice.

My fears heightened the morning after the package appeared when the first e-mail to greet me was from luedtke@clu.edu. Luther Luedtke was the president of Cal Lutheran University,

My first reaction was, "Boy, he didn't like my idea and was writing to tell me to mind my own business."

I was pleasantly surprised when I opened the e-mail. Luedtke said he had read my column, liked my idea, and said the college would go ahead and become the permanent home of the Ventura County Sports Hall of Fame artifacts.

I worked with Eich to come up with an idea to complete the mission.

It was decided that the college would create computerized logs which would include a photo of all of the inductee plaques and other pertinent facts of the Ventura County Sports Hall of Fame.

It would be housed in the new athletic center that the college was building.

I was pleased with the college's decision, and was even more amazed that it took one column and one day for a column idea to come to fruition, a far cry from the more than one hundred columns and eleven years it took to get a state track facility built in Boston.

The Day Ted Williams Tipped His Cap

When the Red Sox announced that they were holding a Ted Williams Day in 1991, I immediately bought two box seats on the first base side of Fenway Park for the big day. I knew the ceremonies would be held in front of the Red Sox dugout.

I was fortunate to see Williams play his final seven seasons with the Red Sox. It was like watching royalty because Williams was one of baseball's greatest legends.

I often told my son David of the exploits of Williams, but Williams rarely made appearances at Fenway. So I was excited for the opportunity to have my sixteen-year-old son see him in person.

After Williams spoke on his special day, he did something he had never done before—he tipped his cap.

The crowd at Fenway rose to its feet, cheered and howled for minutes.

My son seemed baffled by the reaction of the crowd.

"Why are they cheering so loudly?" he asked.

"Son, you are watching history," I smiled.

Despite a brilliant Hall of Fame career, Williams often sparred with the Boston media and sometimes with fans. He responded in many ways, one of which was refusing to tip his cap.

On September 28, 1960, Williams played his final game of his career, against the Baltimore Orioles. In his final at bat, Williams hit a home run off Jack Fisher. In typical Williams fashion, as he crossed home plate, he didn't tip his cap.

Manager Mike Higgins gave Williams one final chance to show his appreciation by sending Williams back into the field for the ninth inning. Higgins then sent Carroll Hardy out to left field, requiring Williams to jog to the dugout. Williams remained true to himself and didn't tip his cap.

When the Red Sox hosted the 1999 All-Star Game, the usual pre-game introductions concluded with Williams being driven to the mound in a golf cart. Both the National and American League All-Stars surrounded Williams and briefly chatted with him.

During that celebration, Williams tipped his cap again.

While the capacity crowd cheered and millions at home watched, I could only think back to that day in 1991 that my son and I had viewed the "historic" tip of the cap.

Wilt Vs. Russell, An Intense Rivalry

When Wilt Chamberlain died on October 12, 1999, I immediately thought of all the games he had played against Bill Russell.

When Wilt came to Boston to play the Celtics at Boston Garden or when they clashed on the road, I rarely missed a game. As a native Bostonian, I enjoyed seeing Russell lose the statistics battle but win the games and titles.

At Wilt's death, I was an assistant sports editor at the *Ventura County Star,* and my readers were Lakers fans. Wilt had concluded his stellar career playing for the Los Angeles Lakers.

I know I wanted to write a column on the Wilt vs. Russell rivalry, still considered the greatest on-court rivalry in the history of the NBA. I didn't want to be accused of East Coast bias, which a lot of people on the West Coast often cried when it came to ratings and comparisons, etc.

I needed an angle for my column that would respect the rivalry without showing favoritism.

It didn't take me long to come up with the perfect approach.

As I began to think abut the super talented pair, the first thing that came to me was that neither Wilt nor Russell had ever played a bad game against each other. They were all-time giants who came to play every game. Even superstars have bad outings now and then, but not Wilt or Russell.

You wanted to always root for your home team against either Wilt or Russell but you had to admire and respect each player's talent, desire, and dedication.

Wilt, who once scored one hundred points in a game, won the numbers battle. In his career, Wilt scored 31,419 points (30.1 points per game), had 23,924 rebounds (a 22.9 average) and dished out 1,643 assists (4.4 per game).

On the other hand, Russell scored 14,522 points, had 21,60 rebounds and 4,100 assists.

Wilt was the ultimate scorer and Russell was the quintessential defender, blocking shots, intimidating shooters, and grabbing rebounds and starting the fast break.

Russell's Celtics won seven of eight playoff series against Chamberlain's Warriors, 76ers, and Lakers teams, and went 57–37 against them in the regular season and 29–20 in the playoffs.

Russell's teams won all four seventh games against Chamberlain's—the combined margin was nine points.

Chamberlain outscored Russell 30 to 14.2 per game and outrebounded him 28.2 to 22.9 in the regular season, and also in the playoffs, he outscored him 25.7 to 14.9 and outrebounded him 28 to 24.7.

Russell and Chamberlain were friends in private life. Russell never considered Chamberlain his rival and disliked the term, instead pointing out that they rarely talked about basketball when they were alone.

When Chamberlain died, his nephew stated that Russell was the second person to whom he was ordered to break the news.

I'm not sure there will ever be as great an individual rivalry, but I'm glad I had the chance to enjoy two incredibly talented basketball players do battle so often and for so long.

Spotlight Hits Close To Home

I anxiously awaited the release of *Spotlight*, the 2015 movie that chronicled The Boston Globe's Pulitzer Prize-winning series on priest pedophiles in the Catholic Church.

The Globe's Spotlight Team's revelation reverberated not only in Boston but around the world.

I considered it the finest piece of journalism in the long and distinguished history of The Globe, where I worked for sixteen years. I also knew many of the Spotlight Team writers, including Walter Robinson and Steve Kurkjian.

My wife and I were in Boston when the film was released, and I wanted to see it as soon as it came out. We were visiting my wife's cousins in Lexington, Mass., and we headed to Waltham to see the movie on a Saturday afternoon.

The Landmark Embassy movie theater, on Pine Street, replaced the original Embassy Theater around the corner on Moody Street. The new theater was on the site of the former News-Tribune, the Waltham daily newspaper where I launched my newspaper career in 1965.

We found the movie in Theater 5, and when we sat down, nostalgia set in. I was sitting in the area of the paper that housed the sports department and where my desk was located in the second-floor newsroom. The hard-hitting movie was well received by the audience, which applauded loudly as the movie ended.

As we left the movie and headed back to Lexington, we passed Sacred Heart Catholic Church, where a colleague of mine had been abused by his parish priest when he was a child.

As we drove past the church, I couldn't help think of the ironies of the day.

Meeting The Yankees' PR Director

Planning a sports trip is so much simpler in the Internet age. Preparing for the baseball trip for my son and me in 1992 was a lot harder.

Today, checking schedules, buying tickets, getting directions, and reserving hotel rooms is just a click away. Twenty-five years ago, planning was a lot harder.

I was fortunate to work in a newspaper where we had season schedules for the major and minor leagues, so schedules were not a big problem. Our local AAA office provided TripTiks for directions, and calls to 800 numbers solved hotel reservations.

There was no such thing as TicketMaster or Stub Hub in 1992, but I wanted to buy tickets in advance so we wouldn't run into long lines at stadium box offices or sold-out games at Baltimore's new stadium, Camden Yards, and Toronto's popular Skydome.

I wrote each team's public relations director, requesting two tickets for the day(s) we were going to be at each stadium. I enclosed my credit card and the request that the tickets be mailed to me.

Within a month, I had received all the tickets with the exception of those for the Yankees-Seattle Mariners game on July 9.

I called Yankees Public Relations Director Jeff Idelson to find out why he hadn't sent my tickets.

"I can't charge you for the tickets," Idelson told me. "I grew up in Newton and delivered *The News-Tribune* when you were writing for the Tribune. Later, I delivered The Globe when you were at The Globe. So, you see, that's why I can't charge you for the tickets."

I explained to Idelson that The Globe had strict policies about accepting gifts, "but given the circumstances, I understand."

I told Idelson I wanted to meet him, and when we arrived for the Yankees-Mariners game on July 9, I called the press box. Idelson came down and chatted with my son, David, and me.

Facing future Hall of Famer Randy Johnson, the Yankees scored six runs in the first inning, aided by four walks, an error, and a hit batsman, and held on for a 7-6 victory.

I haven't seen Idelson since that day, but I did send him a congratulatory e-mail when he was named president of the Baseball Hall of Fame on April 15, 2008.

The Greatest NBA Game Ever

As a young Celtics fan, I often walked up to the Boston Garden box office, plunked down $1.50 for a ticket behind the basket, and watched many a Celtics game.

Even with all the championships won by the Celtics, it was still possible to buy tickets before each game. Because the Celtics didn't always sell out, I often moved down to better seats than the ones I had purchased.

On the night of June 4, 1976, I had the best seats ever, right on the floor of press row. I was covering Game 5 of the NBA Finals between the Celtics and the Phoenix Suns. *Salem News* colleague Gary Larrabee was a regular at Celtics home games, but because this was the Finals, I came along to write a sidebar and notebook on the game.

A year before, I had covered what many considered the greatest World Series game in history, the Red Sox's dramatic 12th-inning victory over Cincinnati in Game 6. Carlton Fisk's homer ended the game at 12:34 in the morning.

When we sat down for the Celtics-Suns game for the 9 p.m. start, thanks to CBS, little did we realize that this game would end after midnight, too.

It was a pivotal game in the series, tied at 2, because if Phoenix won that night, it could wrap up its first NBA title while thwarting Boston's bid for a 13th NBA crown.

There was an unacknowledged timeout at the end of the first overtime that, had it been granted to Boston's Paul Silas, would have resulted in a technical foul and give the Suns a chance to win the game. But referee Richie Powers chose to ignore the signal, and the teams played on.

In the second overtime, Phoenix grabbed a one-point lead with four seconds left, but Boston's John Havlicek raced the length of the floor and scored on a fifteen-foot bank shot that brought hundreds of Celtics fans pouring onto the fabled parquet.

After order was restored, the officials put one second back on the clock and prepared to give Phoenix the ball. That's when the Suns' Paul Westphal asked for, and received, a timeout he knew his team did not have.

The strategy resulted in a technical foul, which stretched Boston's lead to two points, but it enabled the Suns to make the inbounds pass from midcourt. Gar Heard caught the ensuing pass, turned, and sank a jumper at the buzzer to send the game into its third overtime.

With key players on both teams having fouled out, Celtics reserve Glenn McDonald rose to the occasion. He scored six points in the third OT to lead Boston to an exhausting 128-126 win in what was a three-hour, eight-minute thriller.

The game ended after midnight, and when Larrabee and I left the Garden to return to Salem and file our stories for that afternoon's paper, we had seen and covered what many believe to be the best and most exciting NBA game in history.

Two days later, the Celtics defeated the Suns, 87-80, in Phoenix to wrap up their 13th NBA championship.

ABOUT THE AUTHOR

BOSTON NATIVE LARRY AMES, SEVENTY-THREE, WAS A sports journalist for forty-one years.

He worked for *The News-Tribune* in Waltham (Mass.) from 1965-1974, *The Salem (Mass.) News* from 1974-1978, and *The Boston Globe*, where he was assistant sports editor from 1978-1994. He retired in May 2006 as sports editor of the *Ventura County Star* in California.

He was also a part-time sports information director at Bentley College and Brandeis University and was a specialist in the Massachusetts Army National Guard, serving in the 26th Infantry Division's Public Information Office.

Ames was a member of the board of advisors of the Red Auerbach Youth Foundation and chaired the foundation's Leadership Scholarship program. He also served on the board of directors of the Bay State Games.

During his time at The Globe, Ames increased the number of All-Scholastic teams from twenty-five to thirty-six. He also created the Globe Scholar-Athlete program in 1986.

In 2003, The Globe honored Ames by naming the Division 2 and Division 4 Scholastic Awards in his honor.

Ames spearheaded an eleven-year effort to build a state track facility. When ground was broken for the Reggie Lewis Track and Athletic Center at Roxbury Crossing, Ames officially ended "The Track Watch," at 10,852 days.

He was inducted into the Massachusetts Track Coaches Hall of Fame in 1988. The press room at the Reggie Lewis Center is named in his honor. In 2015, Ames was presented with the "Perseverance Award" at a gala celebrating twenty years of the Lewis Center.

The National Football Foundation and Hall of Fame Eastern Mass. chapter honored Ames with the Contribution to Amateur Football Award in 1994. Ames also served on the chapter's Scholar-Athlete selection committee.

Ames was a founding member of the Gatorade Circle of Champions National Board of Advisors and served from 1986-1994 and from 1996-2006.

Ames helped organize the New England Sports Lodge B'nai B'rith chapter All-Scholastic breakfast in 1980 and received the lodge's Lifetime Achievement Award in 1994.

Ames was recognized by the Massachusetts state football, soccer, baseball swimming, track and basketball associations and by the Ventura County (California) Sports Hall of Fame.

Ames was an officer of the Associated Press Sports Editors Association, serving as vice-chair of the West Region for two years and as chair of the West Region for two years.

Ames lives in Camarillo, California, with Bunny, his wife of forty-five years. Their son, David, and daughter-in-law, Stacie, have two sons, Kaden, thirteen, and Vance, eleven.